THE 9ᵀᴴ ANNUAL
ZION NATIONAL PARK
PLEIN AIR ART INVITATIONAL

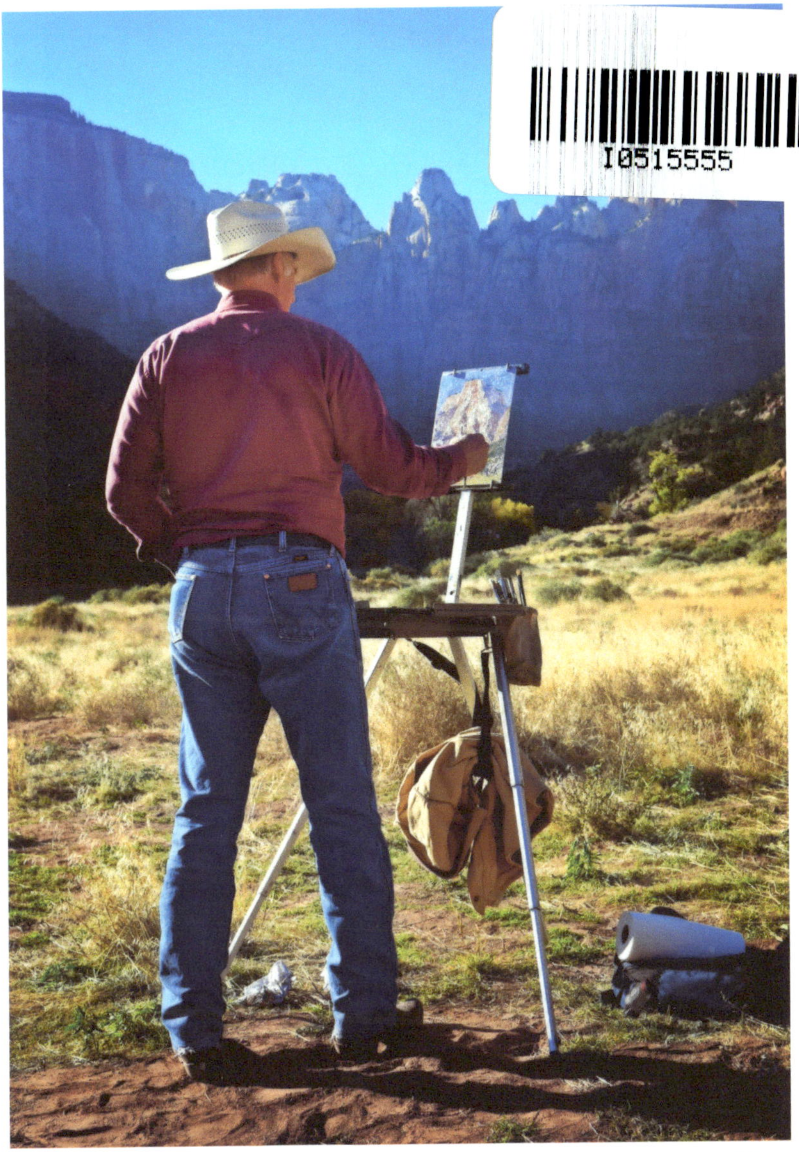

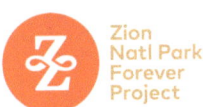

CELEBRATING THE
STORY OF ART IN ZION
NOVEMBER 6-12, 2017

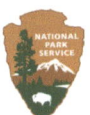

ZION NATL PARK FOREVER PROJECT

Zion National Park
Springdale, Utah 84767
435-772-3264
zionpark.org

Copyright © 2017 by Zion Natl Park Forever Project
All Rights Reserved. Published 2017

No portion of this book may be reproduced in whole or in part, by any means (with the exception of short quotes for the purpose of review), without permission of the publisher.

Printed in the United States of America

Designed by Wade Wixom

ISBN-13: 978-1978249615
ISBN-10: 1978249616

The paintings by invited artists presented in this booklet are representative of the artists' work and are not in all cases plein air paintings. Both studio and plein air paintings are presented, and though some may be on exhibit and for sale in the 2017 Zion National Park Plein Air Art Invitational, their appearance in this booklet does not mean they will be part of the show or sale.

Front cover: James McGrew's *Eternal Majesty* is the featured painting for the 2017 Zion National Park Plein Air Art Invitational.

Title page: Kimbal Warren paints the Temples and Towers of the Virgin.

CONTENTS

5

INTRODUCTION

9th Annual Zion National Park Plein Air Art Invitational

7

THE STORY OF ART IN ZION
Lyman Hafen

12

INVITED ARTISTS

Joshua Been **12**	**36** John Lintott
Arlene Braithwaite **14**	**38** James McGrew
John D. Cogan **16**	**40** Meredith Nemirov
Michelle Condrat **18**	**42** Aaron Schuerr
Bill Cramer **20**	**44** Steve Stauffer
Cody DeLong **22**	**46** Gregory Stocks
Bruce Gómez **24**	**48** Paula Swain
George Handrahan **26**	**50** Michele Usibelli
J. Brad Holt **28**	**52** Kimbal Warren
Mary Jabens **30**	**54** Ellie Wilson
William Scott Jennings **32**	**56** Suze Woolf
Shanna Kunz **34**	**58** William Wright

60

FEATURED PAINTING DEMONSTRATION

Eternal Majesty
by James McGrew

62

ABOUT ZION NATL PARK FOREVER PROJECT

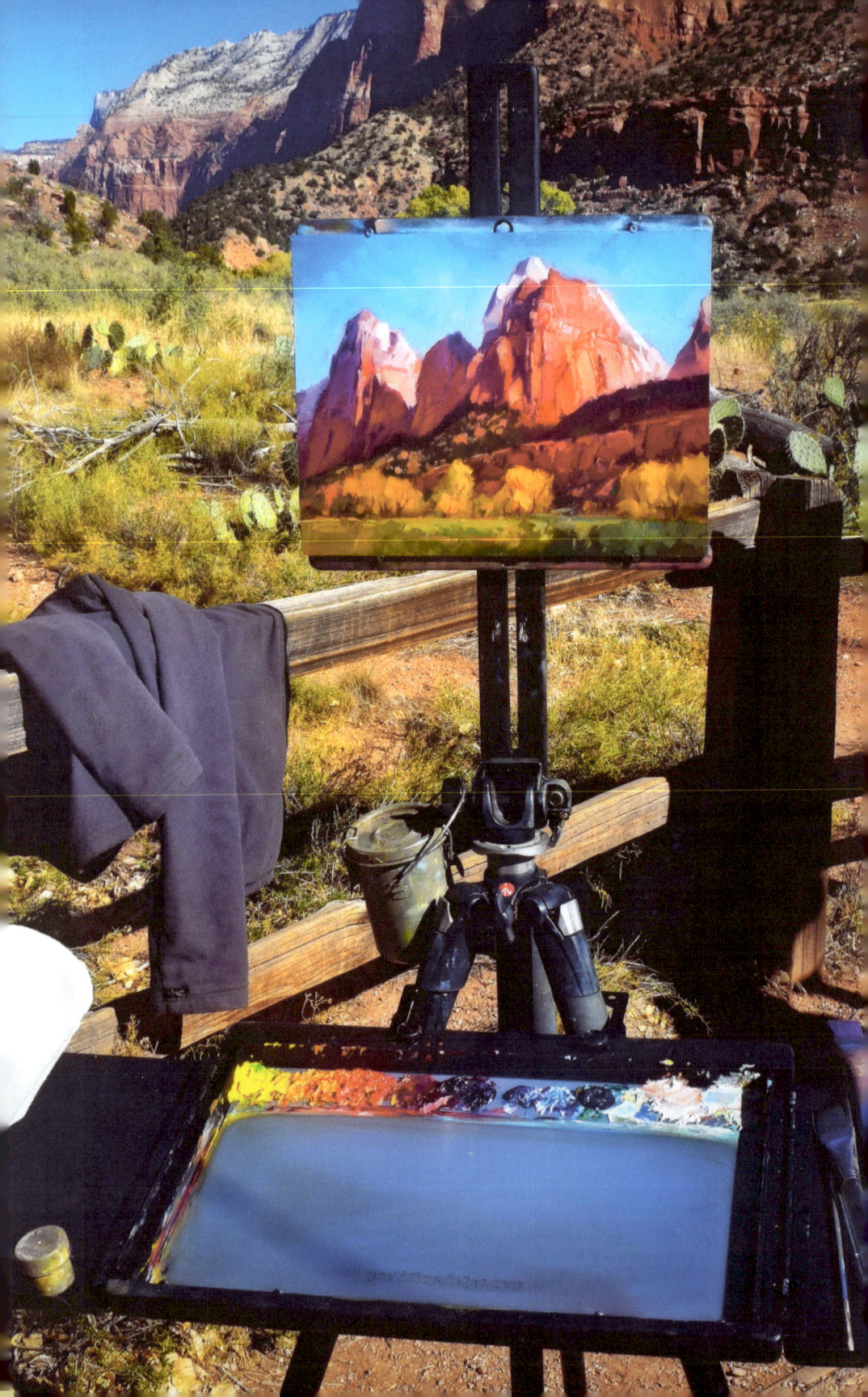

INTRODUCTION

By Mark Preiss
Director
Forever Project

In this setting of canyon, plateau, ancient water seeping from rock and hanging gardens, it is difficult to adequately describe the power this sanctuary holds to inspire millions of visitors every year.

Come November, under angled sun and golden cottonwoods, we bring together twenty-four of the finest landscape artists in the country – to carry on the great tradition of creating art in Zion. Through their mediums, their artistic expressions, we are given the gift of inspiration and deeper meaning. A confluence of creativity and perspective that articulates many responses to this first paragraph.

The event celebrates the role art has played in the creation and history of the park, following in the footsteps of Frederick S. Dellenbaugh, whose first paintings of the canyon, exhibited at the St. Louis World's Fair in 1904, people did not believe existed in real life.

This is Zion's signature event, an extraordinary experience that features all twenty-four artists painting throughout the park, daily painting demonstrations, curated lectures, and a three-day public exhibit and sale of the work produced during the week.

Most of the artworks included in this year's catalogue are studio pieces produced by the artists in advance of the event. Many are on exhibit and for sale at the Human History Museum. All proceeds from the event benefit the park's education and youth initiative programs.

Left: Gregory Stocks work-in-progress at the 2016 Plein Air event on the front patio of Zion Human History Museum.

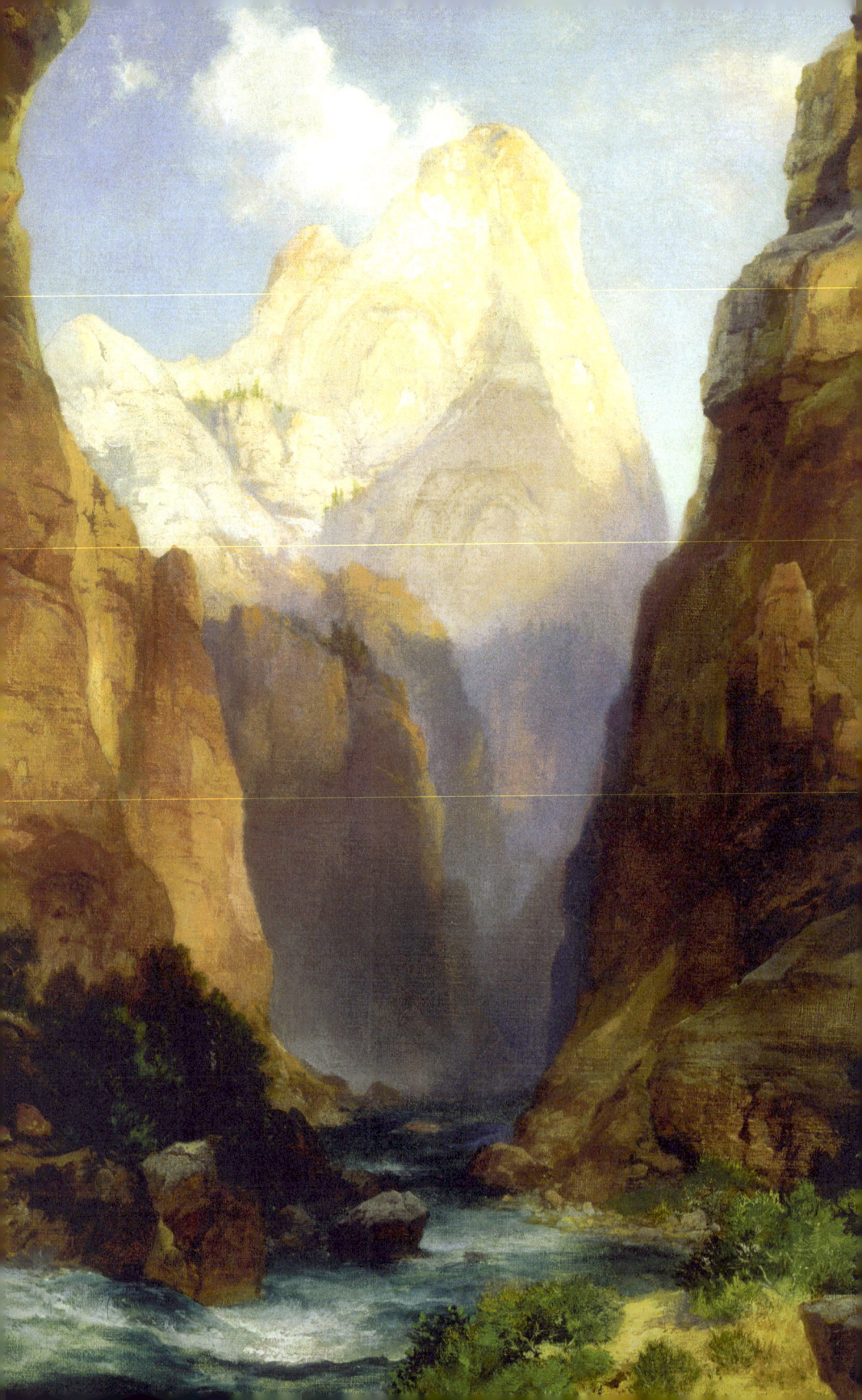

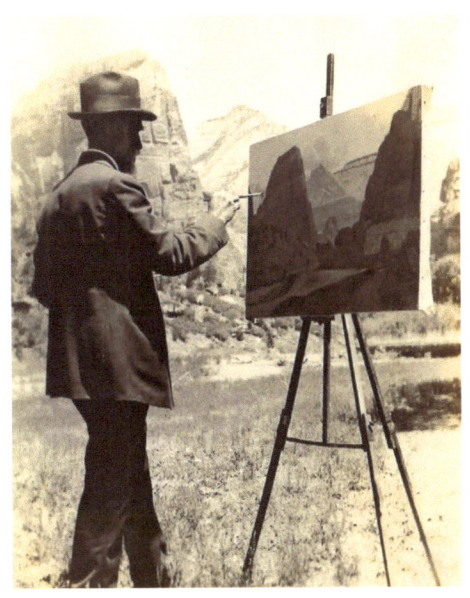

THE STORY OF ART IN
ZION

By Lyman Hafen
Executive Director
Zion Natl Park Forever Project

I once saw a map made in 1857 that covered the western half of the United States. It appeared quite complete except for a blank spot immediately north of the Grand Canyon, including what is now Zion National Park. Of course, the native Southern Paiute people had known and lived in that blank place for centuries, but the early Anglo explorers and mapmakers had not yet ventured into the canyon.

Over the next decade several small Mormon settlements cropped up along the upper Virgin River reaching to the mouth of Zion Canyon, including Rockville and Springdale.

One of those settlers was Isaac Behunin. He ventured farther upstream, built a cabin, and started a farm at what is today the site of the Zion Lodge. During long evenings in the canyon twilight, he would open his scriptures and equate their words with the awesome towers of stone that soared above him. He was the first to call the canyon Zion. For him and the other Mormons who settled there, it was a place of survival and sanctuary.

A few years later others came. They began to discover the canyon for different reasons. With eyes tuned to the beauty and the scientific value of Zion, men like John Wesley Powell, Clarence Dutton, William H. Holmes, Frederick Dellenbaugh, Jack Hillers, Thomas Moran, Charles Savage, and Alfred Lambourne came with the objective of studying it, painting it, photographing it, or writing about it. In the process they fell in love with the place and spared no words, paint, or photographic plates in evoking its beauty, and sharing it with the rest of the world.

Above: John Fairbanks, 1917
Left: Thomas Moran – *The Rio Virgin of Southern Utah*, 1917, 20 x 16 oil on canvas.

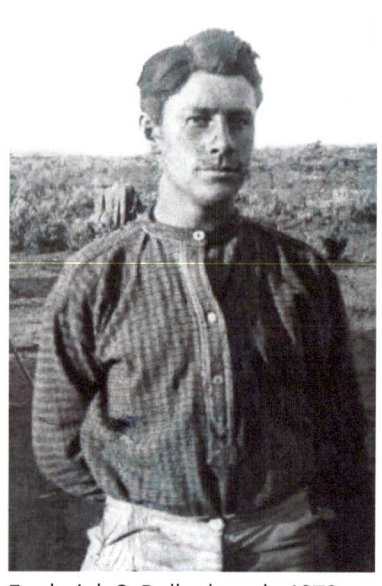

Frederick S. Dellenbaugh, 1872.

Since Thomas Moran first sketched in the canyon in 1873, Zion has been a serious subject for painters. Artists of every medium and style have been coming to the canyon ever since. Today, that legacy is celebrated each year during the first full week of November as two-dozen excellent artists converge in the canyon for the Zion National Park Plein Air Art Invitational.

The fact that a plein air art event would become the biggest annual affair in Zion is no surprise to those who know its history. Art has been a part of its story for centuries, beginning with the prehistoric rock art still visible today in many locations. When the Anglo explorers arrived, they were accompanied by photographers, but the black and white technology of the time could not convey the amazing colors of the canyon to a skeptical public in the east. That's where the work of the fine artists came in. And even their work often fell on incredulous eyes.

In the summer of 1903, Frederick S. Dellenbaugh, who had accompanied John Wesley Powell on his second trip through the Grand Canyon in 1871–72, found his way back to Springdale where he made several forays into Zion Canyon and produced a series of oil paintings that would be exhibited at the World's Fair in St. Louis the following year.

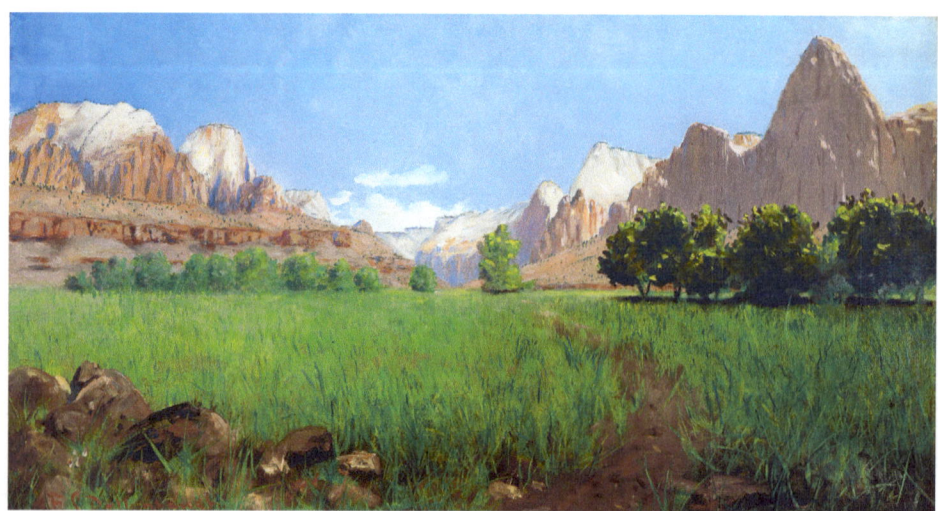

Dellenbaugh's *Zion Canyon*, 1903, 15 x 28 oil on canvas.

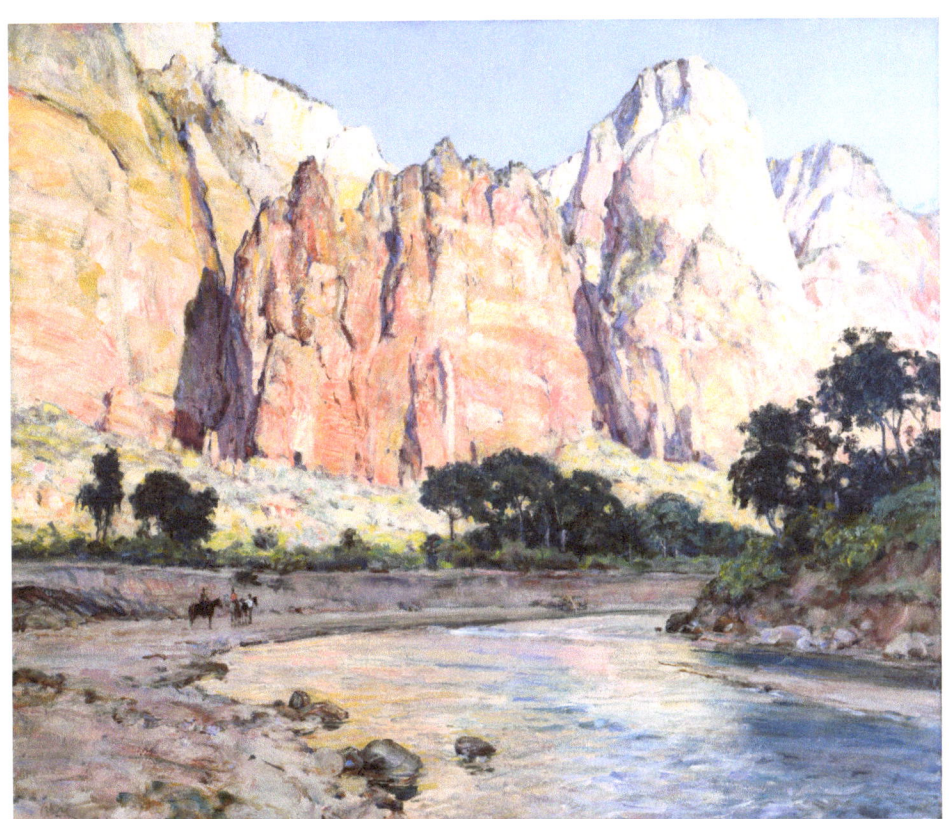

Howard Russell Butler – *Mountains of the Sun*, 1926, 50x60 oil on canvas.

As it turned out, Dellenbaugh's paintings created quite a stir at the 1904 World's Fair. It also happened that a young man named David Hirschi stopped in St. Louis on his way home from an LDS mission in Europe. He had been raised in Rockville, at the foot of the Zion towers, and he knew every hump and hollow of the astonishing terrain surrounding his boyhood home. It was a pleasant surprise to him, as he visited the Utah pavilion, to learn that these wonderful paintings of Zion were a highlight of the fair. But he was alarmed when he saw that many skeptics insisted there could be no such place on Earth, that the paintings must be fake.

Young David Hirschi stood resolute and informed everyone within the sound of his voice that there most certainly was such a place—that he knew its every hill and cliff.

In just five more years David Hirschi's backyard would become Mukuntuweap National Monument, and ten years after that, Zion National Park. The time was fast approaching when people the world over would discover its superlative beauty.

In 2007, through a fortunate series of events, the Zion National Park Foundation was able to purchase one of Dellenbaugh's rare 1904

World's Fair paintings. It had been discovered in an attic in Tennessee and was listed for sale at an antique auction near Knoxville. With barely a week's notice, the Foundation was able to secure funding from the George S. and Delores Doré Eccles Foundation and arrange for a bidder at the auction. Within two weeks, the painting had come home to Zion where it is now part of the park's permanent collection.

The majesty of Zion Canyon has been revealed by countless artists over the years, including the wide mix of 24 artists invited to paint in this year's plein air event November 6-12. The invited artists celebrate the canyon's art legacy by interacting with park visitors as they paint. Each artist will give a one-hour painting workshop in the park sometime during the week, and participate in a public paint-out on the Zion Park Lodge lawn on Saturday. Through the week, the artists create a collection of more than 150 wonderful original paintings. On the weekend, their work goes on sale for the benefit of Zion National Park. And the story of art in Zion continues.

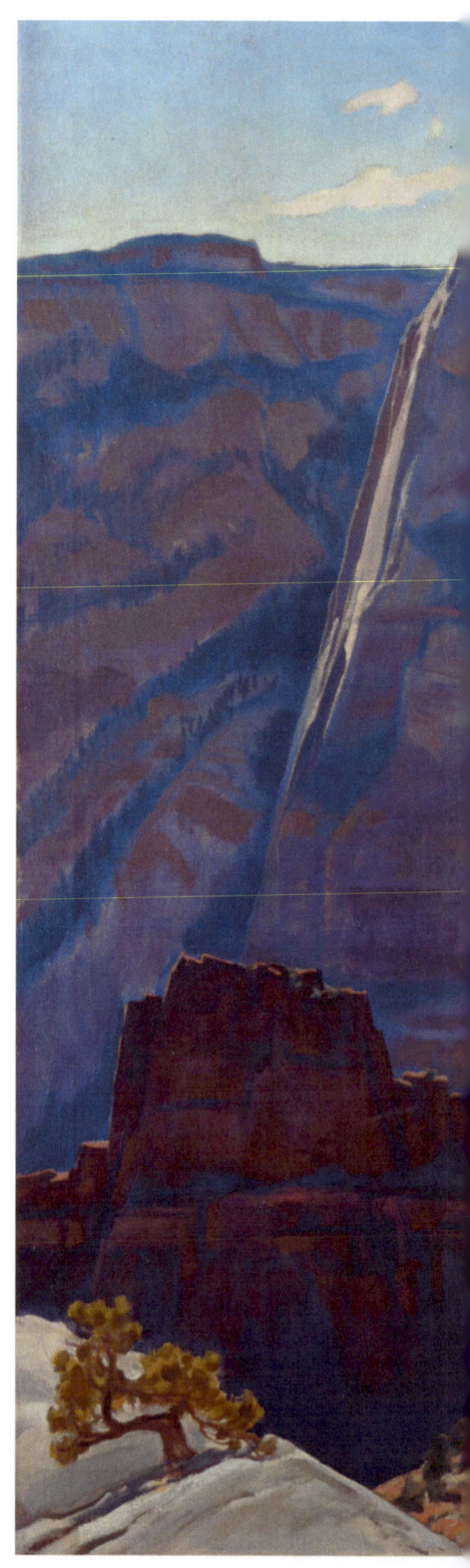

Maynard Dixon – *High in the Morning*, 1933, 36 x 36 oil on canvas, courtesy Brigham Young University collection.

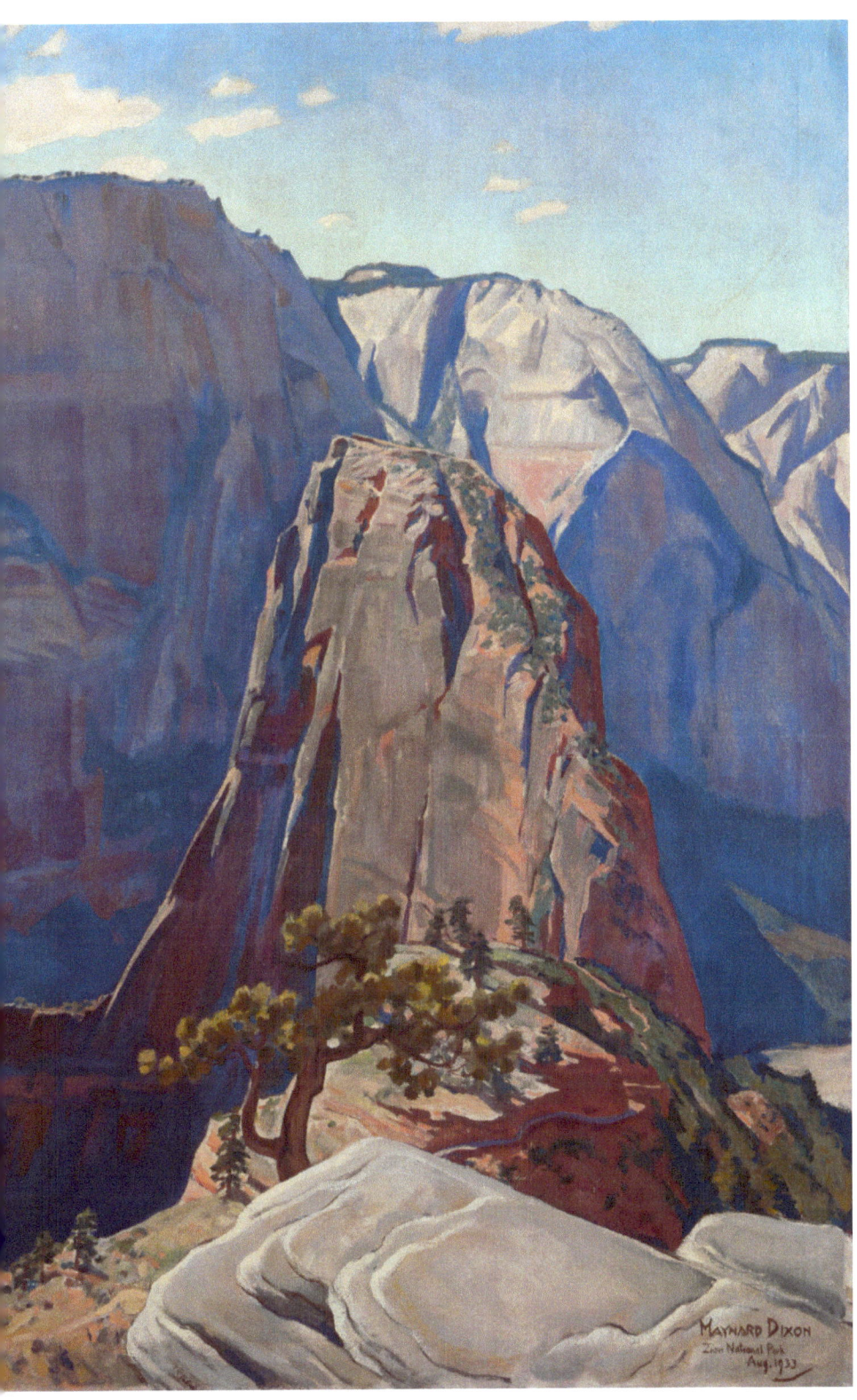

Right: *Virgin River Guardian*
Oil
48 x 16 inches

Far Right: *Rim-to-Rim*
Oil
36 x 12 inches

Vertigo
Oil
30 x 20 inches

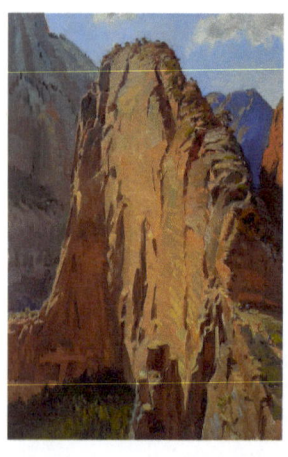
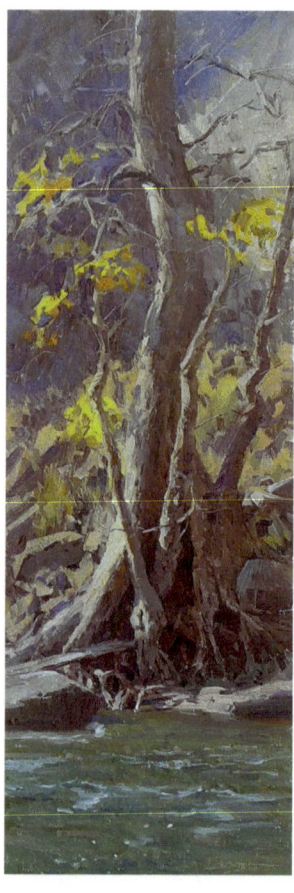
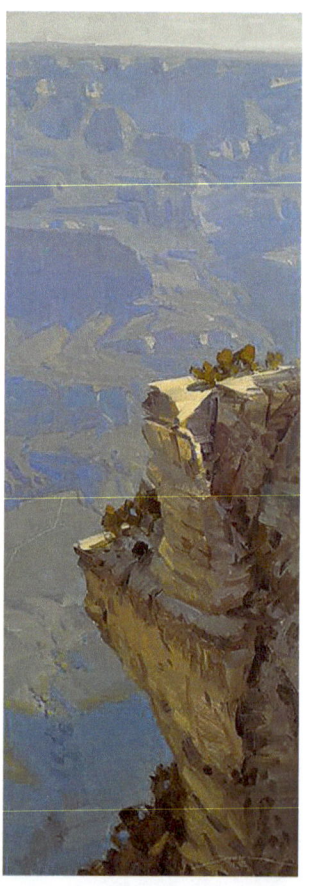
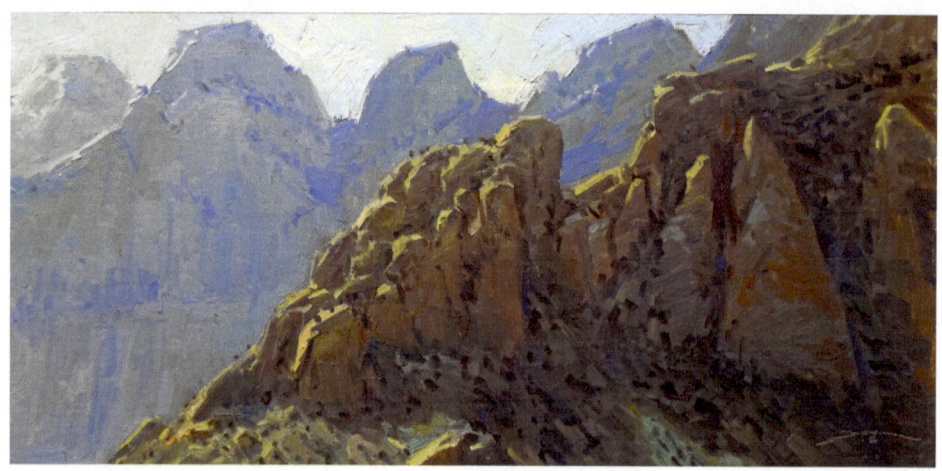

JOSHUA BEEN
SALIDA, COLORADO

"The style I paint is known as Impressionistic Realism. It's a versatile yet challenging mode of expression through which the poetry of a subject is preserved and paramount. To find eternal balance in the elegant dance of light and form is my highest inspiration. Through the congruence of our visual vocabulary and shared human experience, I am able to imply detail without overstating it. . . Through my work, I sincerely hope to remind and inspire others to take time to see just how amazing this existence is."

Joshua Been, born in 1974, had no shortage of outdoor adventures that cultivated his appreciation for the natural world. Drawing since he could manage a pencil, he was captivated by animation and cartooning. This interest remained with him throughout high school and an active duty enlistment in the US Army. Joshua then went on to pursue his BA in Fine Art at Fort Lewis College in Durango, Colorado. As a Magna Cum Laude graduate from this small liberal arts college, Joshua found interest in more than just art classes. He was active in theatre and performing arts, while studying earth sciences as well. This interdisciplinary foundation is evident in the intricacies and truthful fascination of his landscape as well as his figurative work.

A Switchback Story
Oil
20 x 30 inches

Flash Flood Reminder
Pastel
12 x 12 inches

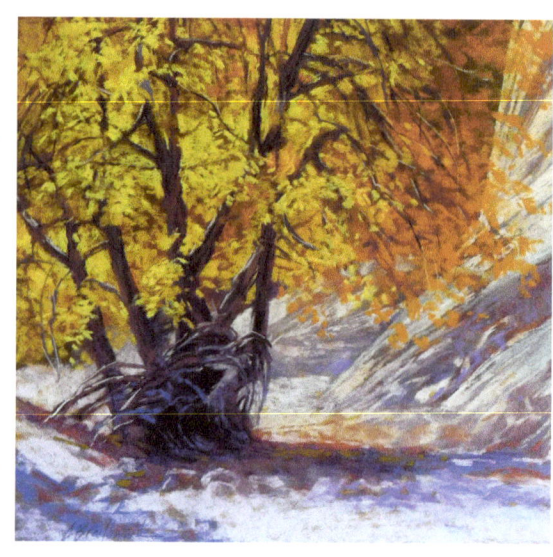

Sunrise View - Angels Landing
Pastel
24 x36 inches

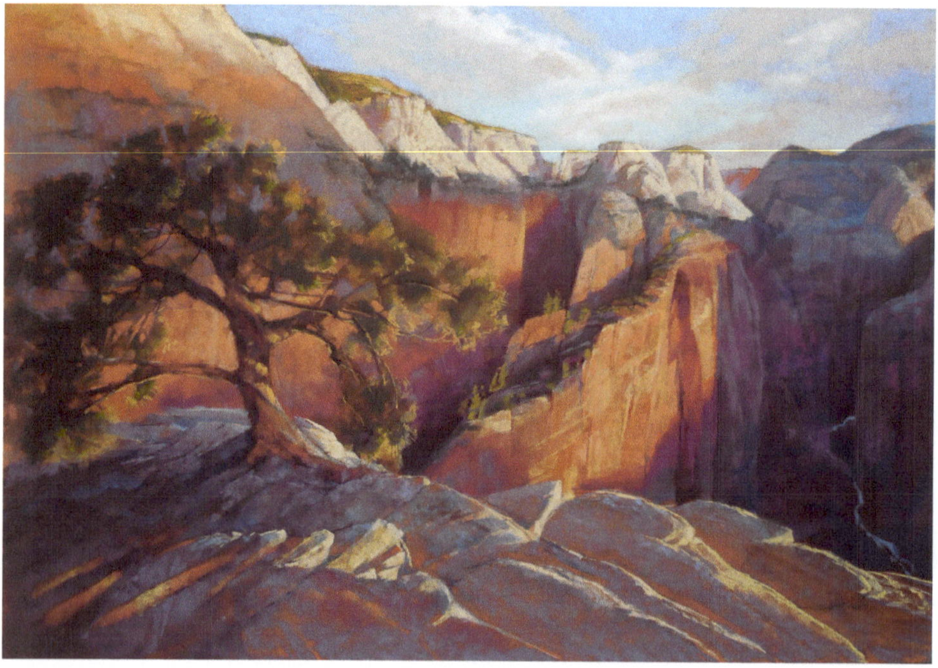

ARLENE BRAITHWAITE
CEDAR CITY, UTAH

"My work is inspired by the land around me, a subject I find continually changing, challenging and rich with catalysts for composition. Pastel is attractive to me because of its immediacy. I enjoy the direct contact with the pigment, and the bold to subtle hue mixtures that can be achieved through hatching and layering pastel. During the painting process I focus on the quality of light, atmosphere, surface textures, shifts in color temperature and edge variations. My goal is to create a painting that will resonate with the viewer's experience."

Pastel painter, Arlene Braithwaite, earned her master's degree from the University of Utah. Upon graduation she enjoyed a 32 year teaching career as an art educator at Southern Utah University. Upon retiring she was able to focus her full attention on pastel painting. Her work has been shown in solo exhibitions at the Springville Art Museum, the St. George Art Museum, the Utah Museum of Natural History, and Zion National Park's Museum of Human History. Arlene's paintings have also appeared in the magazines Pastel Journal and International Artist, and the books Art of the National Parks, Painters of Utah's Canyons and Deserts: Historical Connections Contemporary Interpretations, and Artists of Utah.

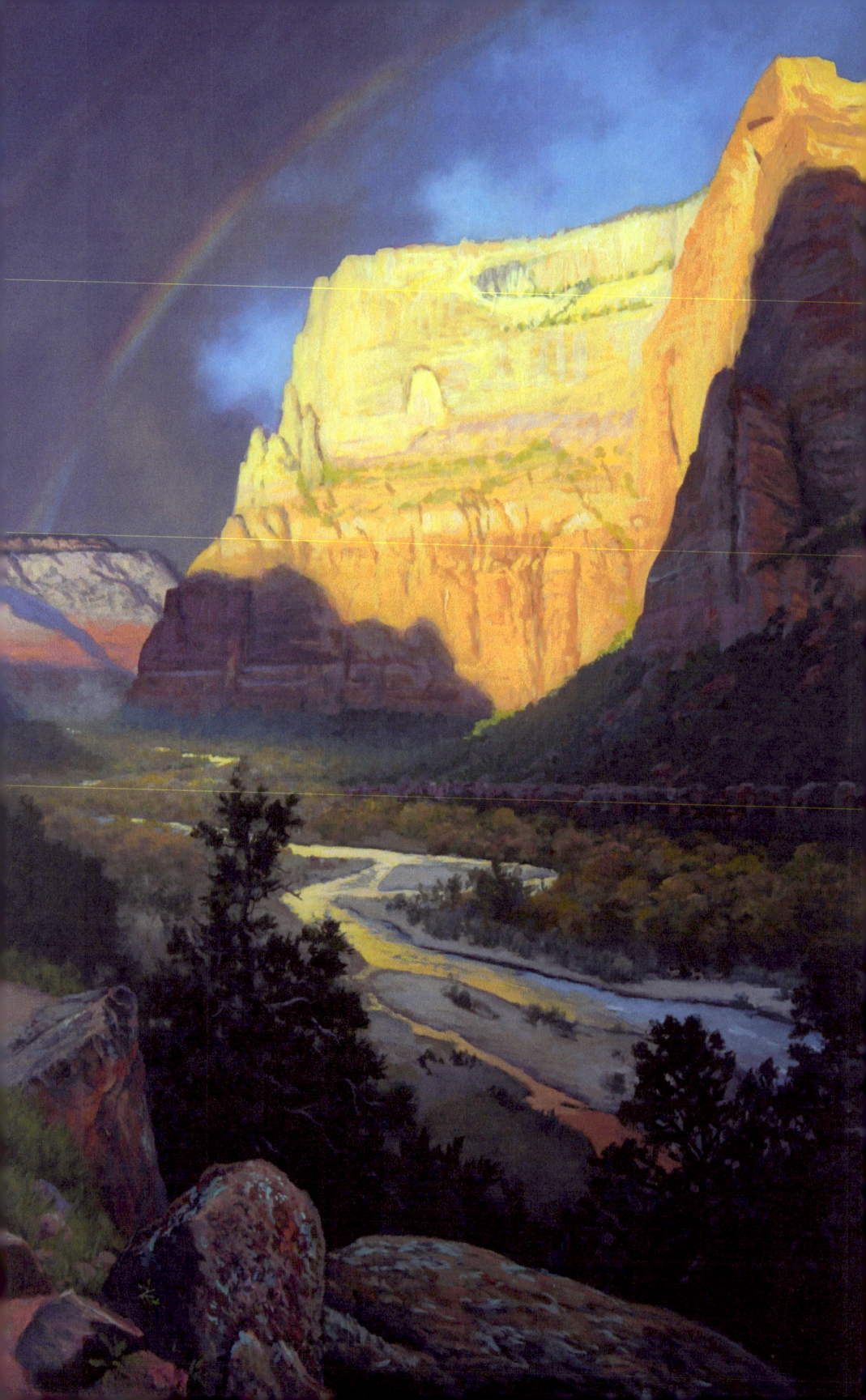

JOHN D. COGAN
FARMINGTON, NEW MEXICO

"The first year I painted in the Zion Plein Air Art Invitational, I wondered if I would find enough subject matter to paint for a week. By the end of that first event, I knew the problem was just the opposite. Now I realize a lifetime is scant time to paint in all the canyons and valleys, on all the trails or overlooks. Even year to year the changing weather and the advent of autumn are so unpredictable that Zion is a new locale all over again. Zion is a lifetime plus of challenges for the plein air painter."

John Cogan captures the beauty of creation on canvas, painting the landscapes of the american west in a unique style that has become known throughout the United States and the world. He paints primarily in acrylic, focusing on color and the effects of light.

John earned a PhD in physics from Rice University in 1981. But he loved painting more than science and by the following year, painting had become his vocation.

Zion National Park is one of John's favorite painting destinations; its quiet beauty and cathedral-like setting have inspired many of his best paintings. He has participated in the Zion National Park Plein Air Art Invitational from 2010 through 2017, winning multiple awards as well as the Superintendent's Award in 2011 and the Foundation Award in 2015.

Golden Throne
Acrylic
24 x 18 inches

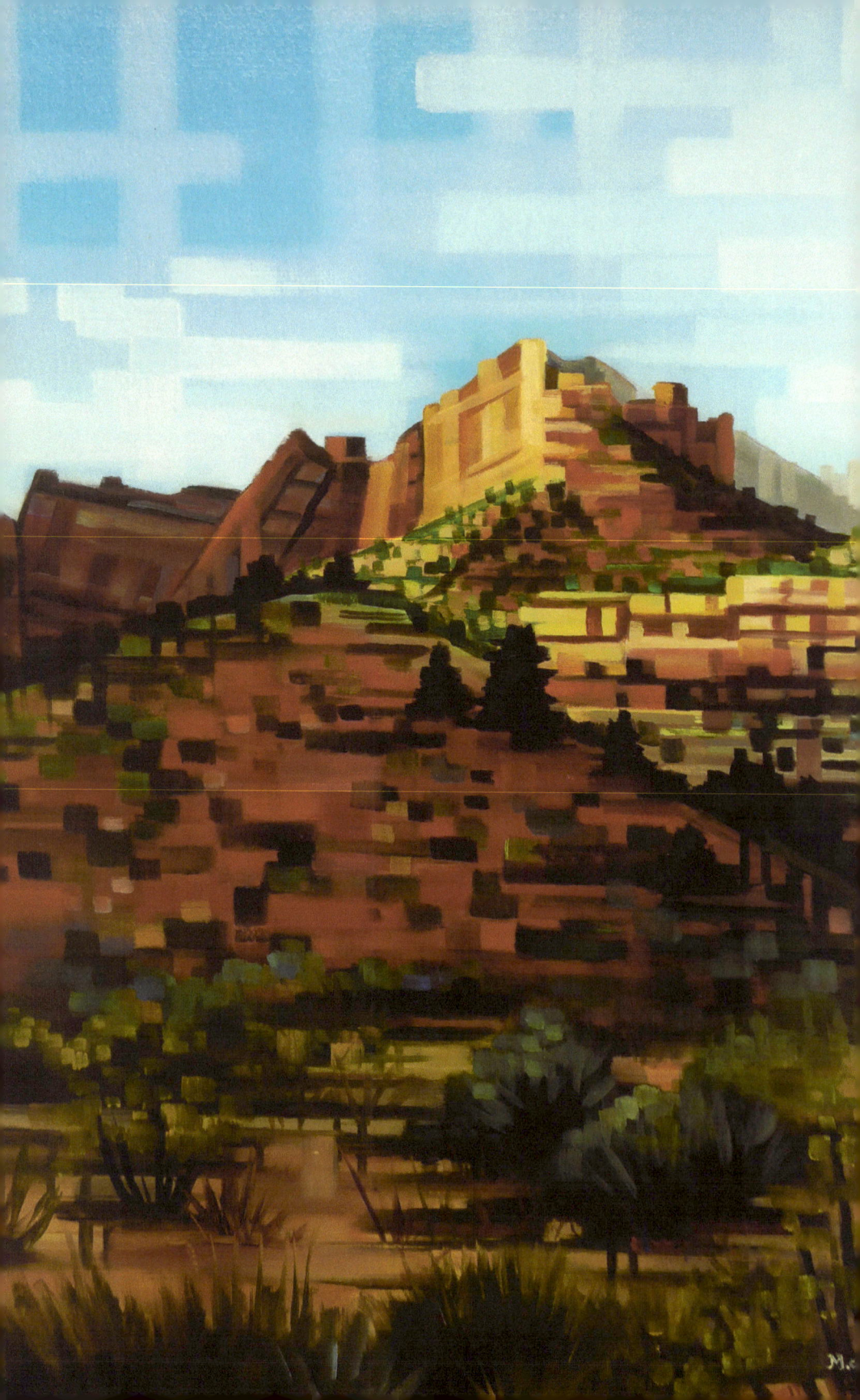

MICHELLE CONDRAT
SALT LAKE CITY, UTAH

"Art cannot be reined in like a wild animal; it cannot be tamed, or trained or told what to do. It is forever changing. It is part of our history as well as our future. As an artist, it is my job to use it for communication, for self-expression, and for public surveillance. Art is power... art is part of who we are . . . art is forever."

Michelle Condrat was born and raised in Salt Lake City, Utah. She graduated from the University of Utah, with a bachelor's degree in painting and drawing and a minor in art history. Michelle enjoys painting the unique landscape Utah and the Southwest offers, and spends a lot of her time in Utah's outdoors, where she gathers inspiration for her paintings. With intense color choices and broad blended strokes, Michelle captures the unique look of the western landscape while creating a fresh visual perspective in her work.

A Lifetime of Happiness
Oil
16 x 12 inches

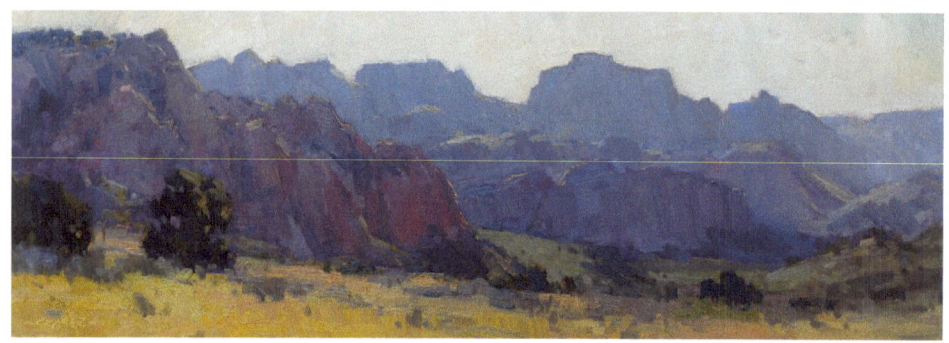

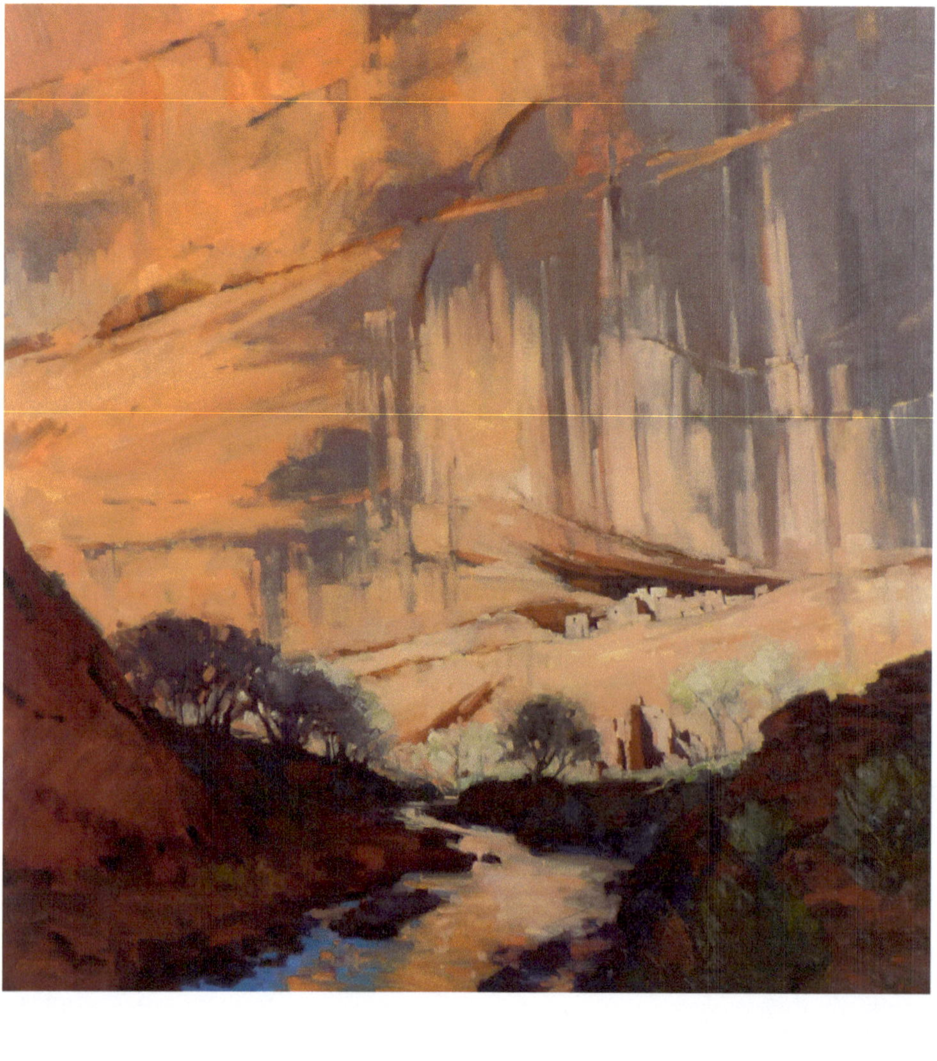

BILL CRAMER
PRESCOTT, ARIZONA

"I truly enjoy the essential act of laying down paint, especially on location. I look for a balance between the actual scene and my reaction to it; not to paint precisely what I see, but to paint what I want the viewer to see. . . The push of an evening breeze, the feel of sun baked sandstone, the scent of sagebrush or the sound of a raven suddenly overhead are examples of the many unseen elements that inform my work. I'm satisfied when a painting is as rich as the landscape that inspired it. My goals are to keep exploring the Southwest's wild places, search for new ideas and express what I find exciting about landscapes and about painting."

Growing up in southern California, Bill always had an interest in exploring nature and creating art. As an experienced rock climber, he spent much of his youth enjoying the more vertical places of the american west. This gave him a perspective of the world that few others would ever experience. He received a fine arts degree from California State University Long Beach in 1989. He later moved to Prescott, Arizona with his wife Michelle to be closer to the scenery they both enjoyed. It was there that Bill discovered the joys and challenges of landscape painting, his outdoor experiences providing much of the insight and inspiration expressed in his art.

Cave Valley Cruisin'
Oil
8 x 24 inches

Path to the Ruins
Oil
36 x 36 inches

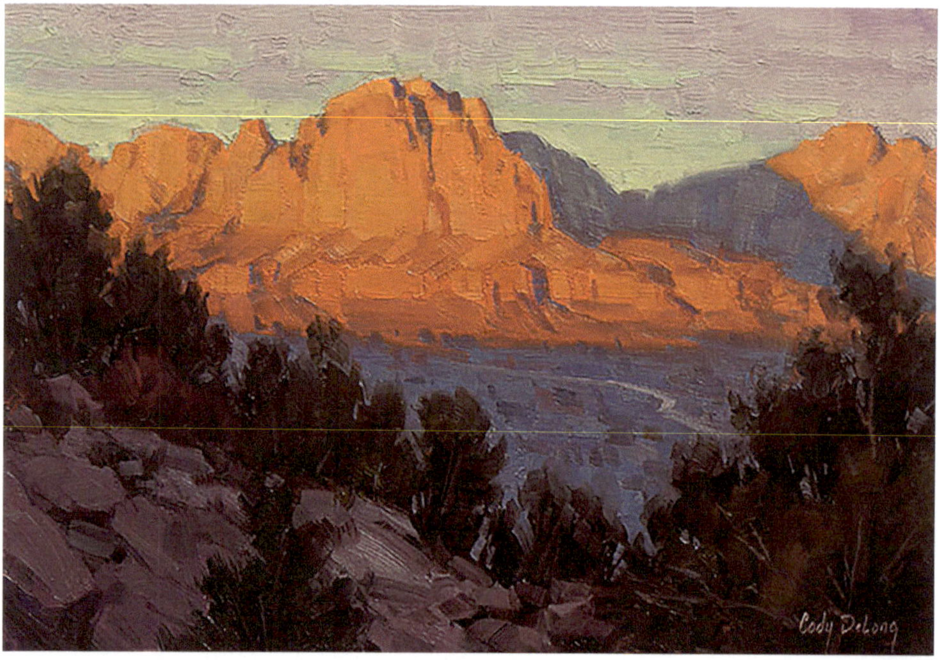

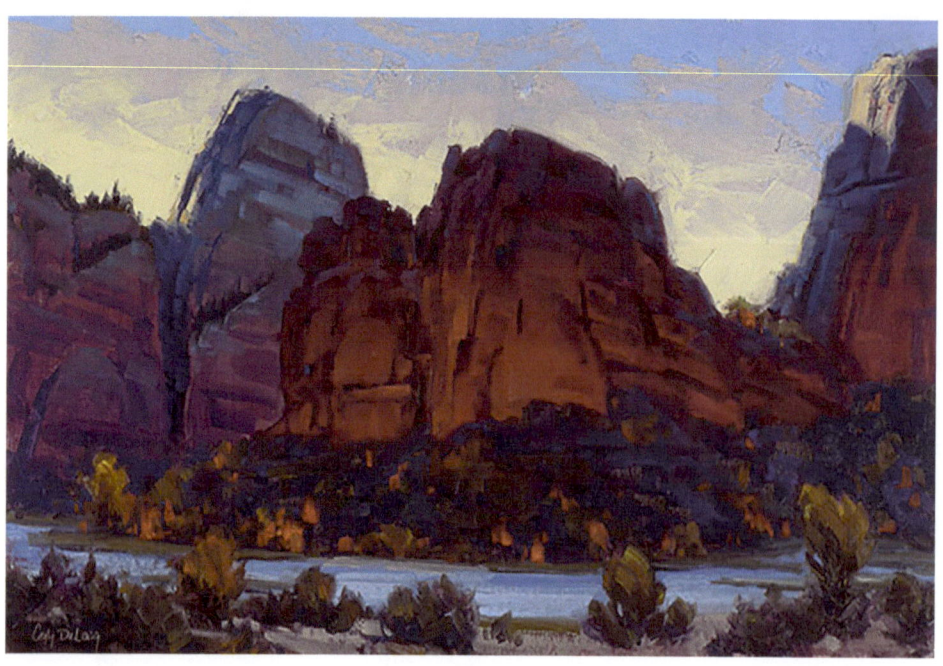

CODY DELONG
COTTONWOOD, ARIZONA

"Each painting I do springs from an idea I have about my subject. I'm not a formulaic painter, meaning I don't use the same approach for each painting I do. This is a sometimes risky way of working, but it's what keeps my love alive for the process. I feel like I can never learn it all, so each new day is an opportunity to challenge myself to grow in new directions. The end result hopefully, is painterly, with great color, light and drama. I hope to catch your eye and make you think differently about the scene, and perhaps, about painting."

A lifelong student of art, Cody has studied at the Loveland Academy of Fine Arts, as well as the Scottsdale Artists School, where in 2003, he was awarded a merit based scholarship. In 2004, the Oil Painters of America selected him as that year's Shirl Smithson Scholarship Winner. In 2009 Cody was awarded a Teachers Scholarship by the Marylin Sunderman Legacy Fund for his innovative workshop techniques.

North to Zion
Oil
8 x 12 inches

Night Turns Into Day
Oil
12 x 18 inches

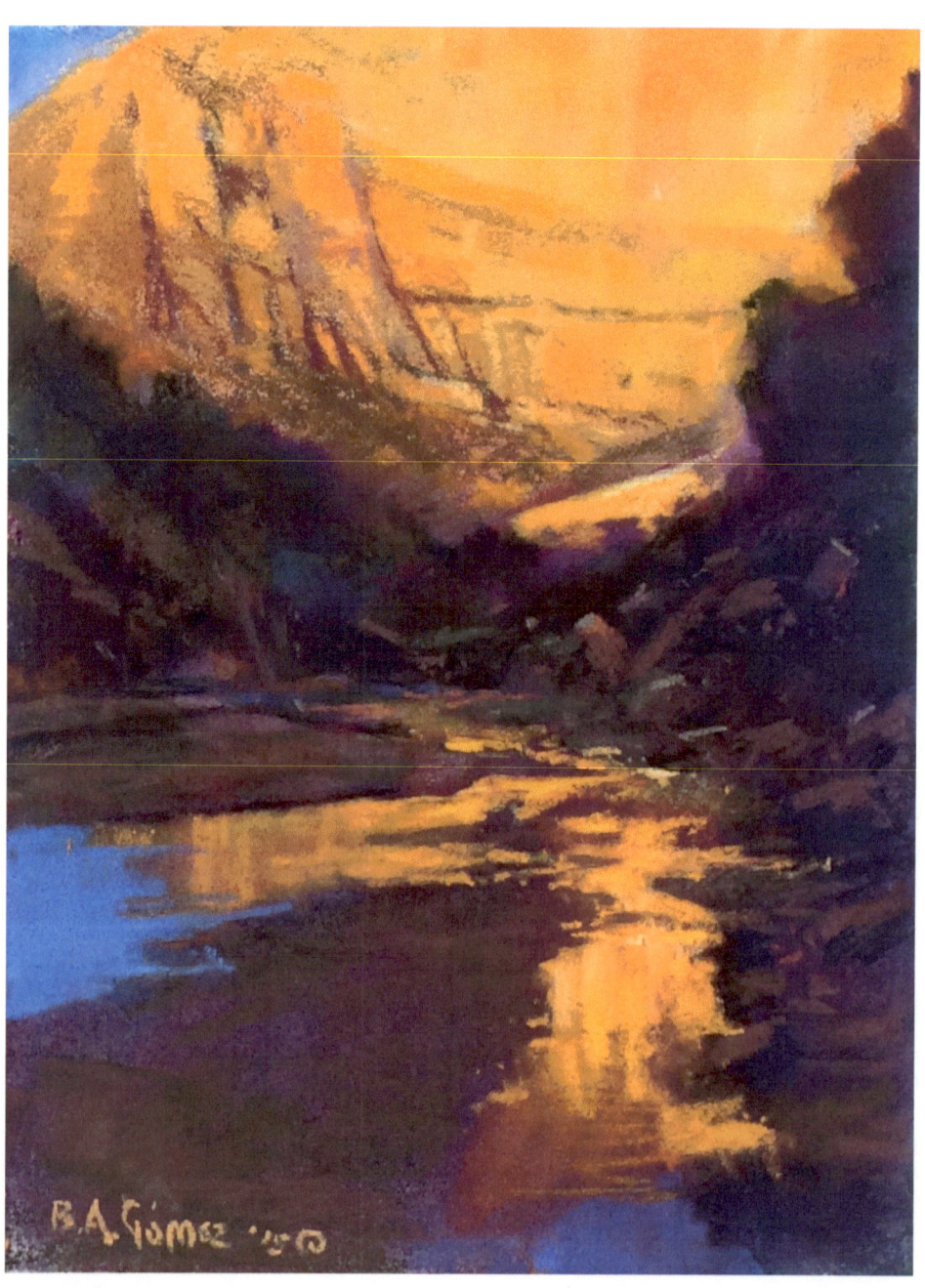

BRUCE GÓMEZ
DENVER, COLORADO

"I have painted full time as an artist for the last 27 years and have really painted as a plein air artist for the last eight years throughout the Southwest and Washington state. My paintings are landscapes although I do urbanscapes as well as floral compositions. I enjoy the challenge of painting in a non-traditional medium - pastels and I feel that even after all these years, I've only just begun to figure out the secrets of this illusive medium."

Bruce Gómez was born in Denver, Colorado in 1957, and was educated at Colorado State University and the University of Colorado at Denver, where he received a degree in political science, as well as a degree in romance languages and constitutional law.
   Bruce is entirely self-taught, and he paints exclusively in pastels. He paints everything from urban images of Denver, New York, London, Paris and Rome to landscapes of Colorado, Utah, Arizona, Montana, and Washington, as well as Tuscany and Provençe. He has produced the artwork for numerous festivals and events, including The Telluride Chamber Music Festival, Telluride Wine Festival, Telluride Jazz Festival, and Sedona Wine Festival. One of his images will be used for Paint The Peninsula Plein Air Competition.

Pine Creek
Pastel
15 x 11 inches

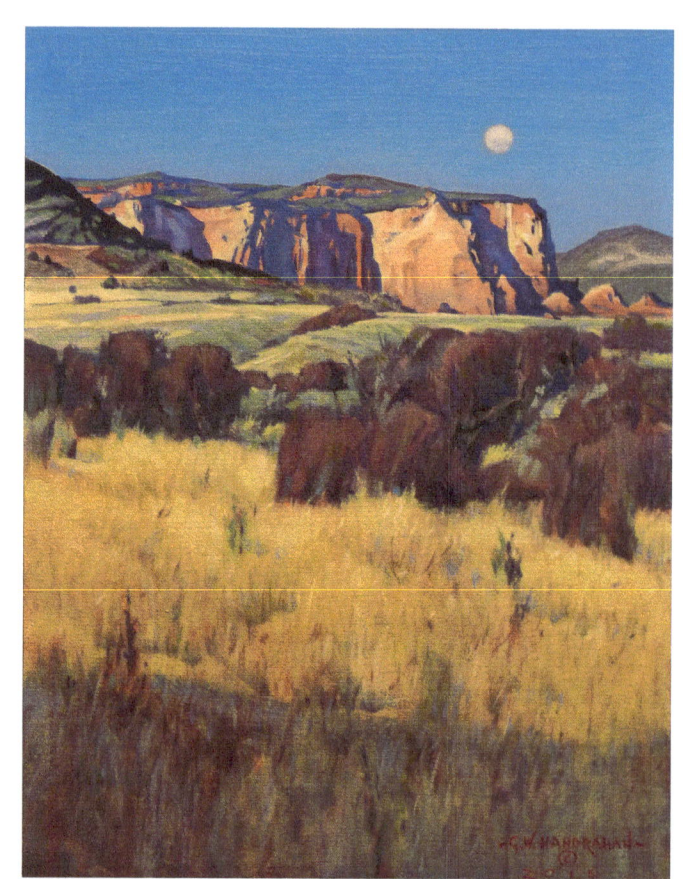

Kolob Moon
Oil
14 x 11 inches

Sunlight & Shadows
Oil
16 x 24 inches

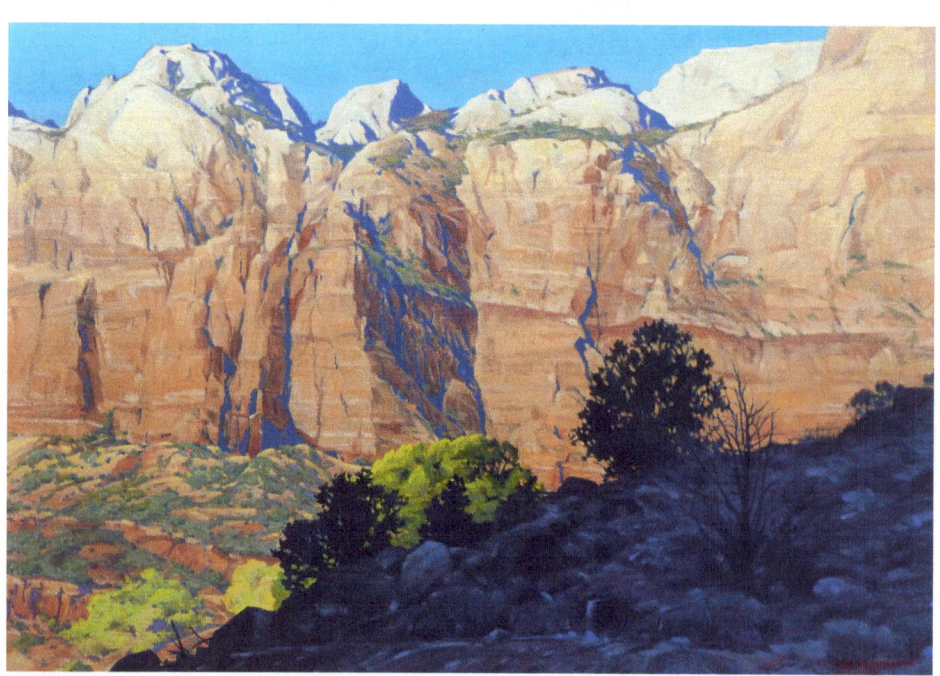

GEORGE HANDRAHAN
LAYTON, UTAH

"My work reflects the life cycle evident in the world we live in – relationships, interactions, contrasts and comparisons - both natural and man-made. It is seeing the dark or the light, the hard or the soft, the mass or the minuscule, the beautiful opposites that make a subject interesting, then communicating these in a unique and expressive way. It's not about making pretty pictures, it's about creating a work with real art value…a real work of art."

George W. Handrahan, a native of Utah, was raised in the rural community of South Weber. It was in this environment that he came to love and appreciate the diverse natural landscape surrounding him, taking every opportunity to spend time out of doors.
   As a student, George learned to appreciate many forms of art but gravitated towards the work of LeConte Stewart, the American impressionists, and artists of California, admiring their ability to portray the essence of light and form. Earning his degree in art from Weber State in 1976 under Farrell R. Collett and Richard Van Wagoner, these influences led him to devote his skills full time to landscape painting. George's art is characterized by both his lifetime affinity with nature and his grasp of the concerns of such artists as those previously mentioned.

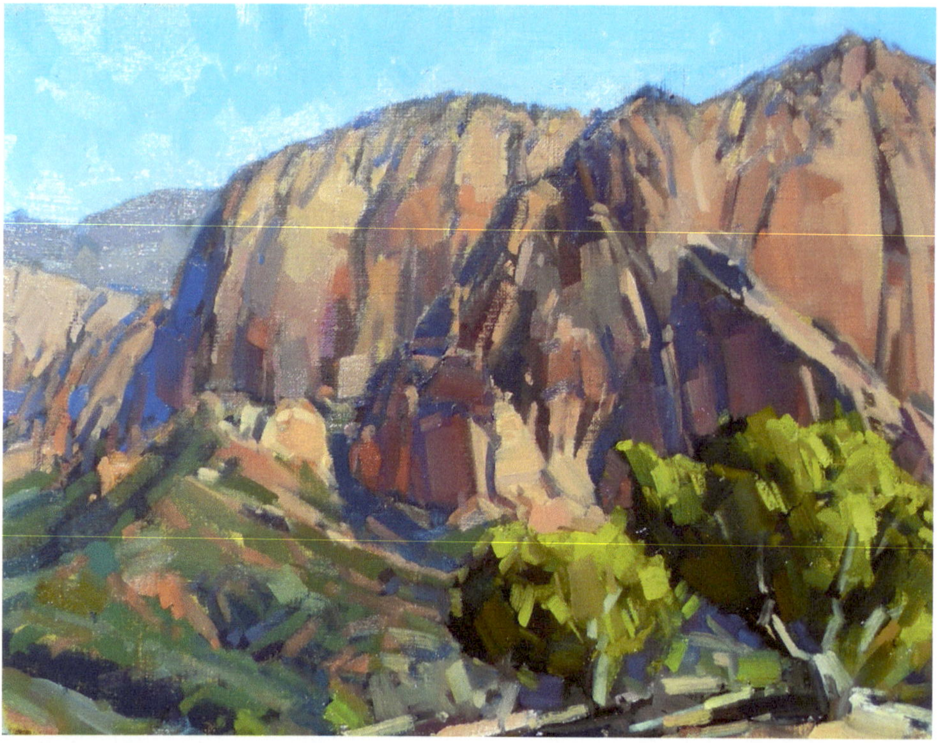

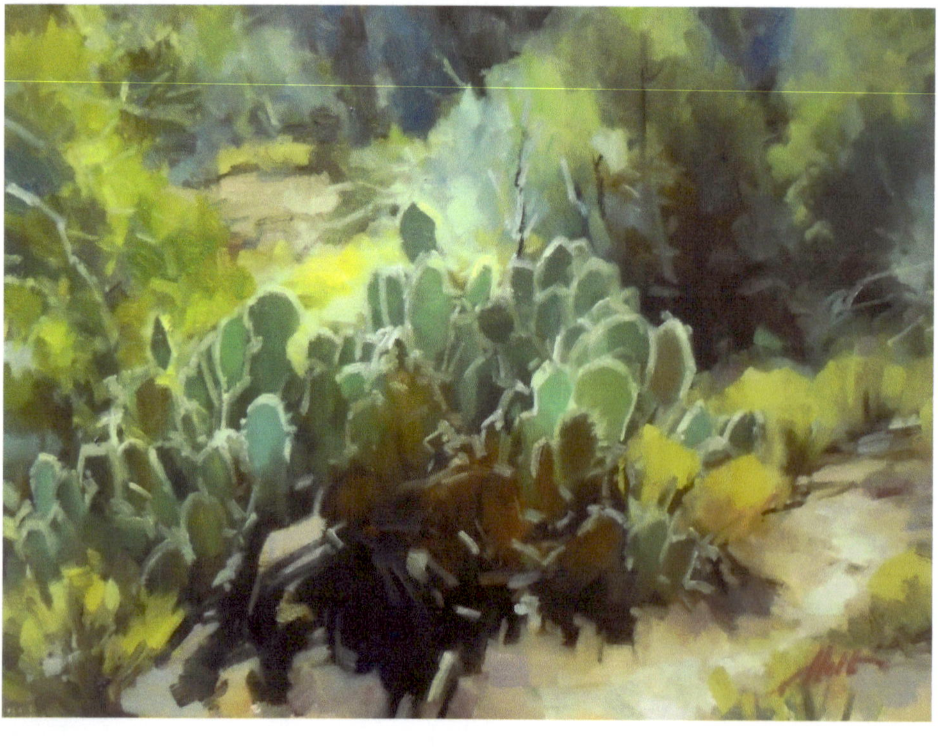

J. BRAD HOLT
CEDAR CITY, UTAH

"One of the guiding motives of the zeitgeist of twentieth and twenty first century art has been the deconstruction of portraiture as part of a general de-emphasis of subject. Representational landscape painting is not immune to this trend. In plein air painting, it manifests as an appreciation of the economy and elegance of the artist's hand, as a manifestation and artifact of his or her intentionality, as well the artist's confidence in their own inner vision. The artist naturally evolves when they grow beyond the idea of likeness, towards brevity, and elegance, allowing representational painting continuing aesthetic relevance in the world of modern, and post-modern art."

J. Brad Holt grew up in Cedar City, Utah. He spent childhood summers working on his grandfather's ranch in Orderville, Utah hauling hay and punching cows. He graduated from Southern Utah State College (now SUU) as an Art Composite major. He spent several seasons as a musician/performer with the Utah Shakespearean Festival in Cedar City, Utah.

Kolob
Oil
9 x 12 inches

Cactus
Oil
12 x 16 inches

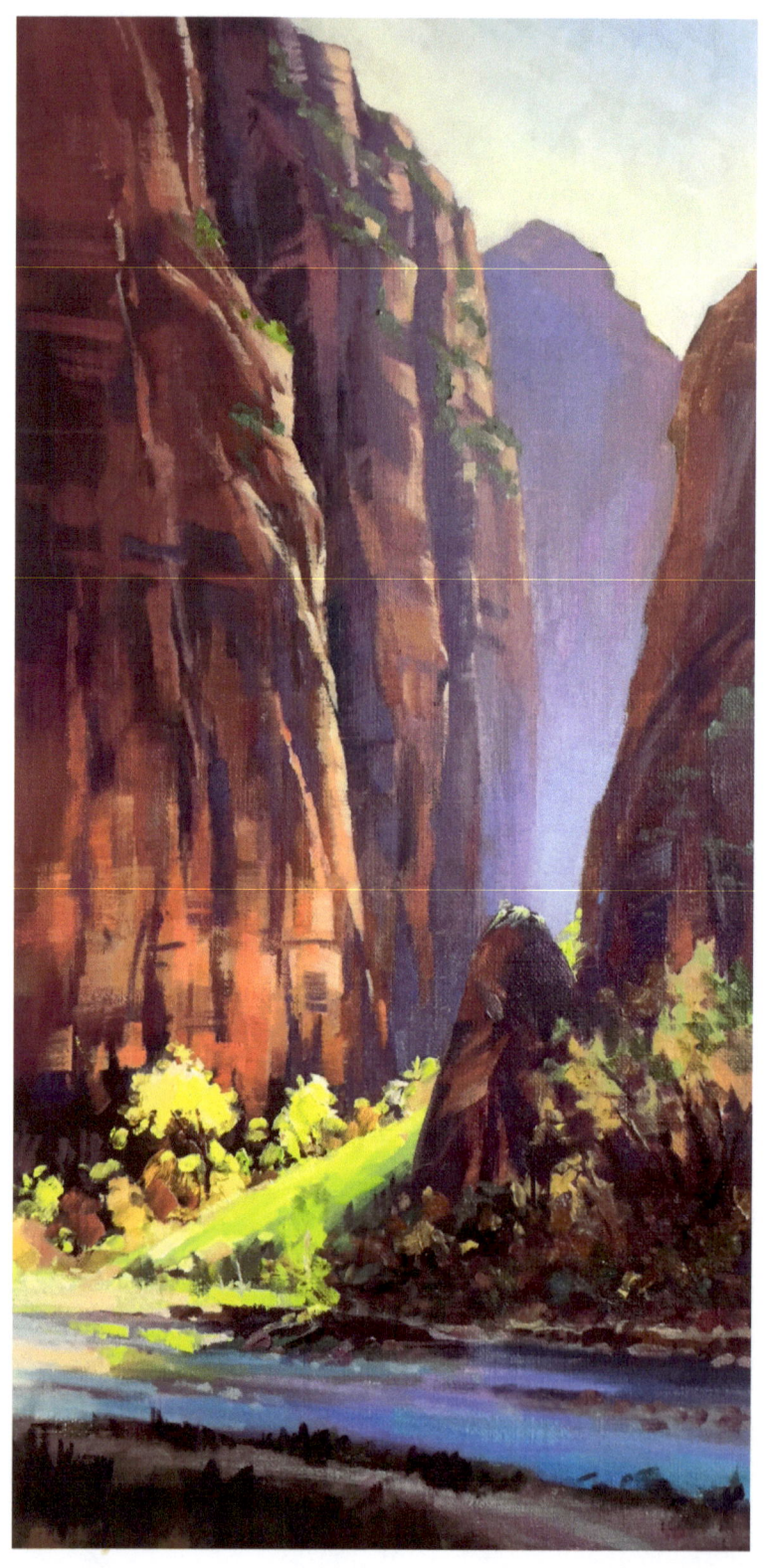

MARY JABENS
CEDAR CITY, UTAH

"My passion is plein air painting. The paintings I love the most choose me. Whether it's a color, shape value or subject - something stops me and says paint. Interpreting what I see in nature and putting it on canvas is a challenge I enjoy. My goal is to communicate with the viewer the joy I see around me. With minimum paint strokes and details, I try to relay an amazingly real experience of the places I love. Painting heals me one picture at a time, replacing the uncertainty of the day with a feeling of hope and goodness again."

Artistic influences in Mary's life are always present in her mind when she is painting. These influences include Thomas Moran, John Singer Sargent, Edgar Payne, and most recently Tibor Nagy and Mark Boedges. She feels that she has been blessed at different times of her life with several mentors who have helped further her artistic ability.

River Walk
Oil
16 x 8 inches

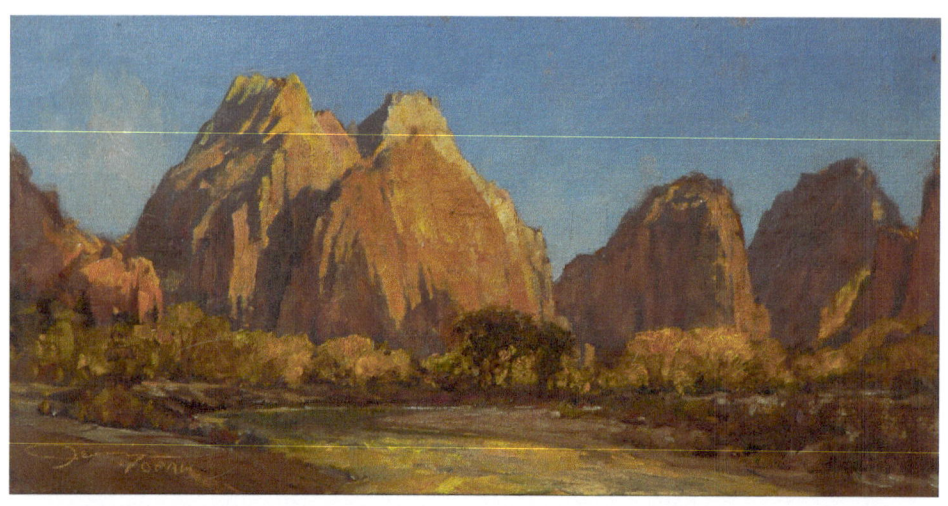

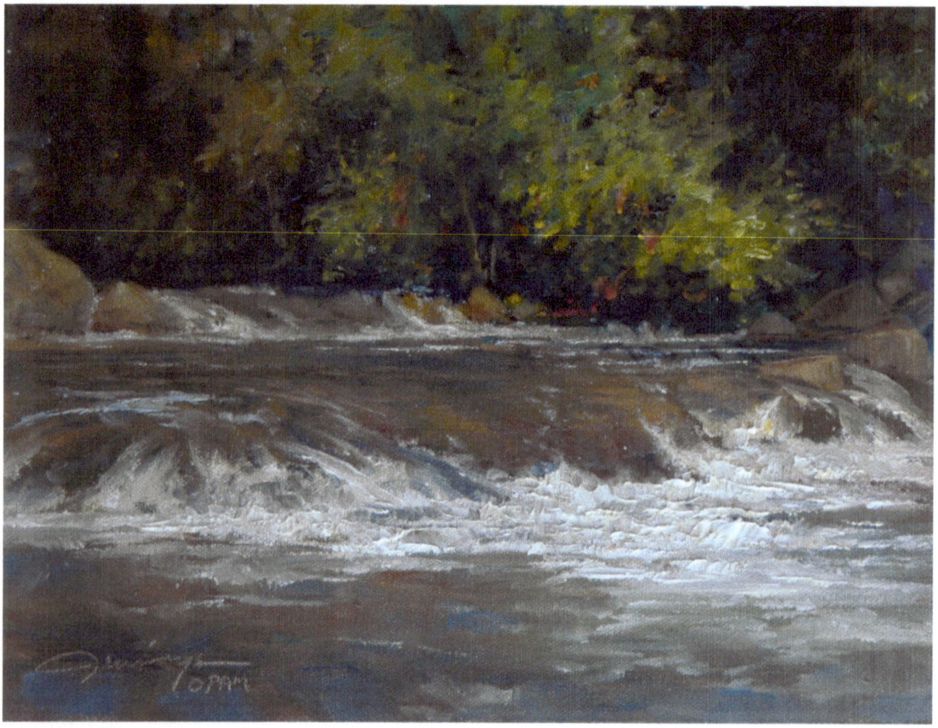

WILLIAM SCOTT JENNINGS
LOUISVILLE, COLORADO

"Photos seldom give the psychogical feeling of a place. It's all there in the photograph, the rocks and the leaves and all that. But you don't get that knot in your stomach of standing on the precipice of a canyon. I'm interested in the psychological feeling of it. That's what it is when I'm standing at the edge of a canyon. It's what I need to have happen before I send a painting out the door."

William Scott Jennings has been a professional artist since 1973. He began his career in commercial art, gallery exposure began in 1976, and by 1978 he was showing his work in New Mexico , Arizona and Texas. Scott moved to Boulder, Colorado in 2009. His paintings are in corporate and private collections around the world, including the U.S. Capitol in Washington, DC and the Ford Motor Company.

Autumn in the Canyon
Oil
8 x 16 inches

Boulder Creek
Oil
12 x 9 inches

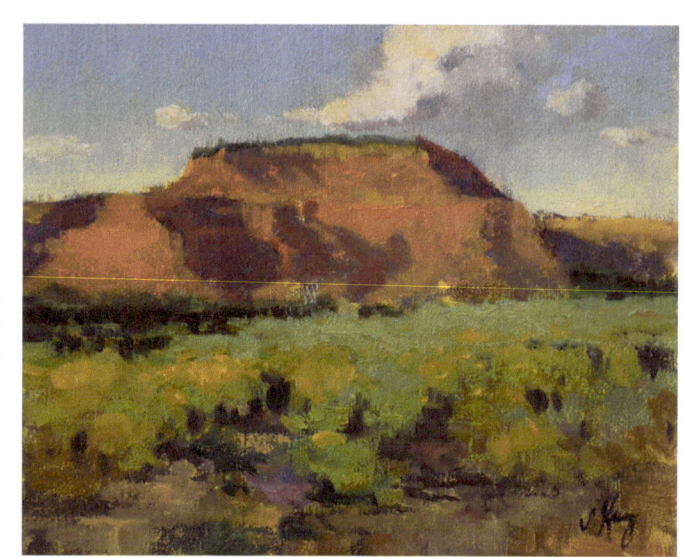

Kanab View
Oil
8 x 12 inches

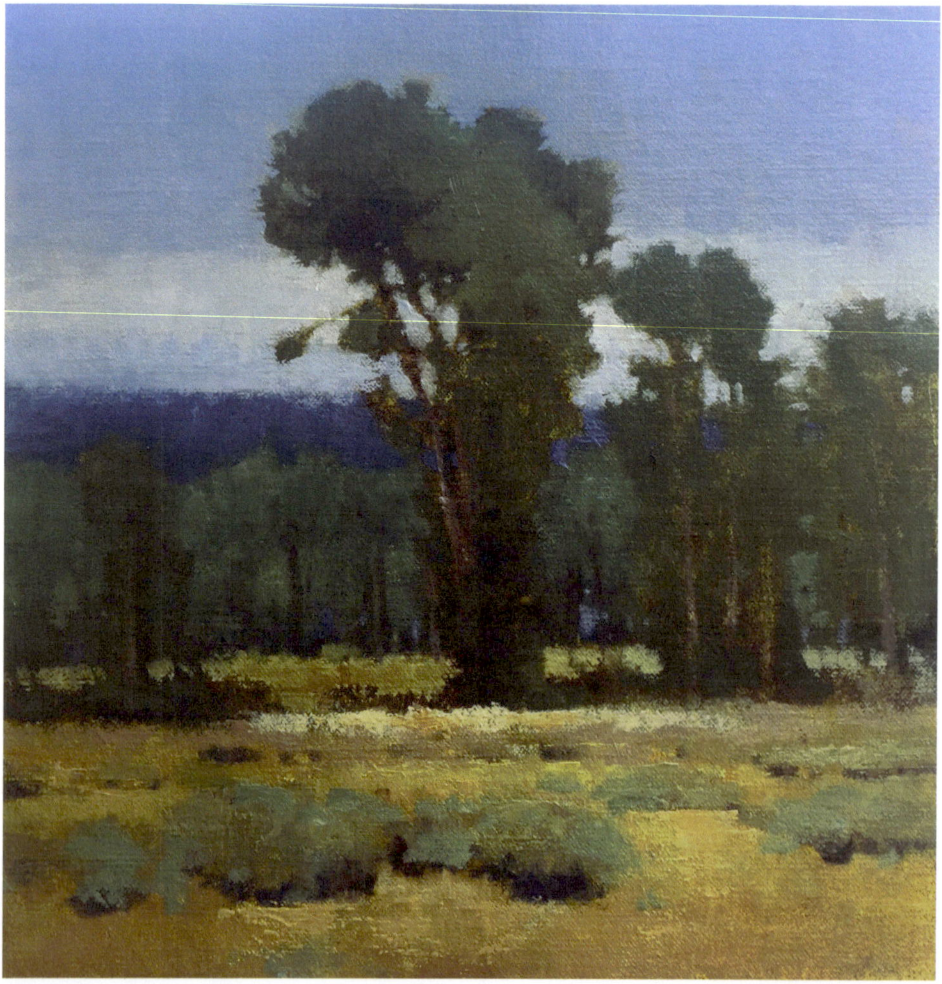

SHANNA KUNZ
OGDEN, UTAH

"As a contemporary landscape painter, my work is a conscious play of mood, light and color, but as a naturalist raised and rooted in the diverse landscapes of western America, a painting means more than that to me. Each location is an encounter with the land, the trees, and the waters that have always given me a sense of connection and order. When a location intrigues and inspires me, I will paint the scene into a series using a range of keys or themes, experimenting and searching to learn more about the natural threads that tie the landscape together with complexity, subtlety and more importantly balance."

Shanna Kunz resides in Ogden, Utah and has painted plein air and studio work in the west for over 25 years. She has recently been featured in numerous major publications, including feature articles in *Plein Air, Outdoor Painter, Southwest Art, Western Art Collector* and *American Artist* magazines. Shanna has participated as a guest artist in The Coors Show, 2014; Maynard Dixon Camp Out 2015 & 2016; C.M. Russell Auction 2015; Rocky Mountain Plein Air Painters as Guest Artist 2016; American Impressionist Society Exhibition 2016; Maynard Dixon Land 2010; the Jackson Wildlife Museum Western Visions Miniature Show; the Contemporary Art of the American West Invitational; The Western Masters Art Show; and was chosen for the Fine Art Connoiseur Award at the Artist of the New Century Exhibit, Bennington Center for the Arts.

Guardians
Oil
36 x 36 inches

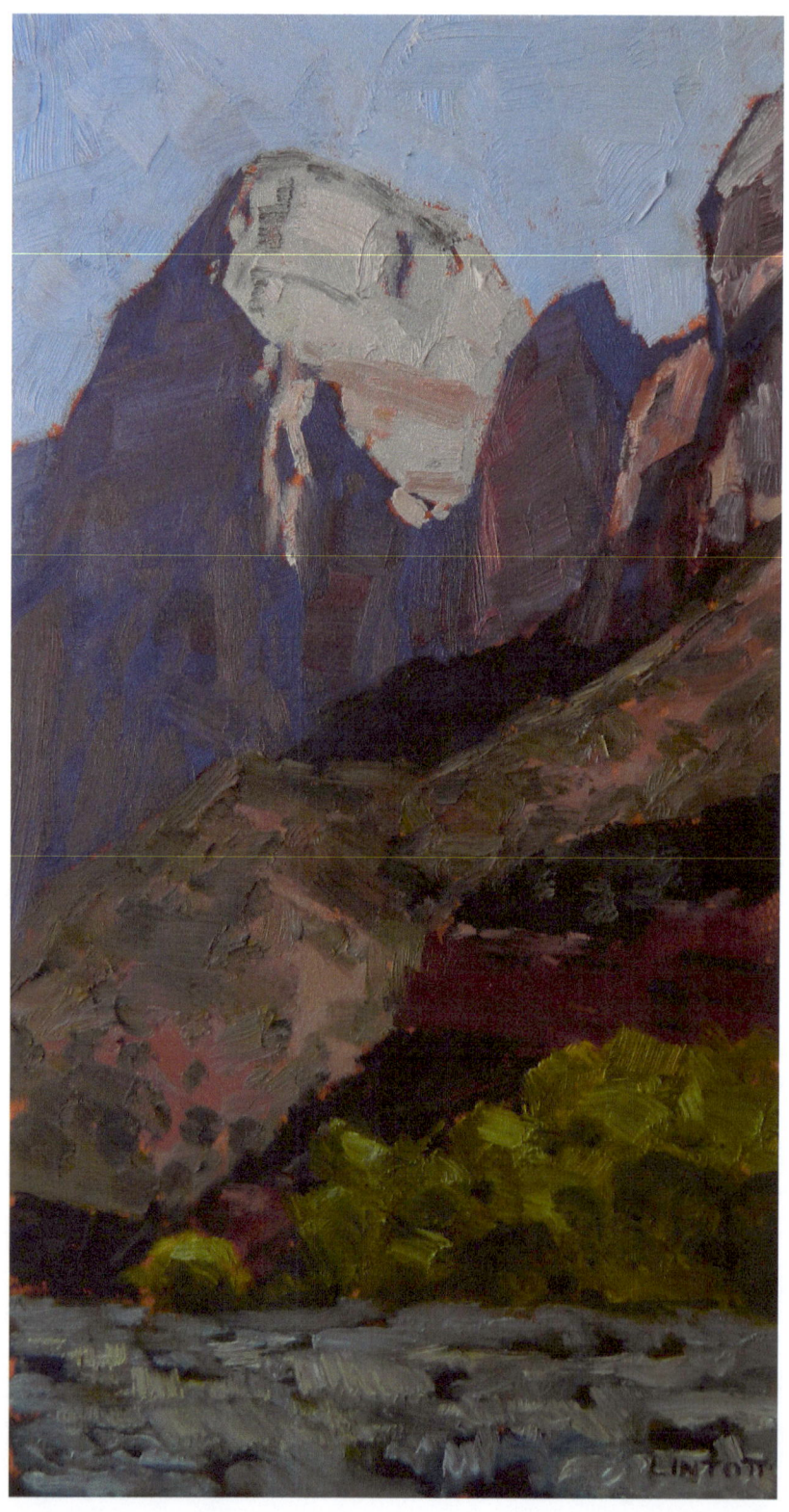

JOHN LINTOTT
GRAND JUNCTION, COLORADO

"I love approaching new challenges in the landscape. Tweaking my process to adapt to new problems forces me to constantly evolve my painting and keeps me interested and passionate about it. Seeking out the beauty and solitude of the landscape is the best way for me to put everything else aside and enjoy the outdoors."

In 2001, John Lintott graduated from Colorado State University with his B.F.A. concentrating in painting. The following year he moved to Fruita, Colorado with his wife, Emily. Working for the family business, John painted at all times available in the evenings and on weekends. In 2007, he and his family purchased a custom frame shop in downtown Grand Junction. For the next 7½ years, John operated the frame shop while turning the front gallery space into his own studio. Ultimately, John decided to close the frame shop in 2014 in order to pursue his true passion of plein air painting and painting in the studio without the distraction of the frame shop. He states, "I realized I needed to commit myself to sketching the world outside directly, as often as possible, in order to truly understand how to approach a larger, more detailed studio painting."

Layers of Light
Oil
16 x 8 inches

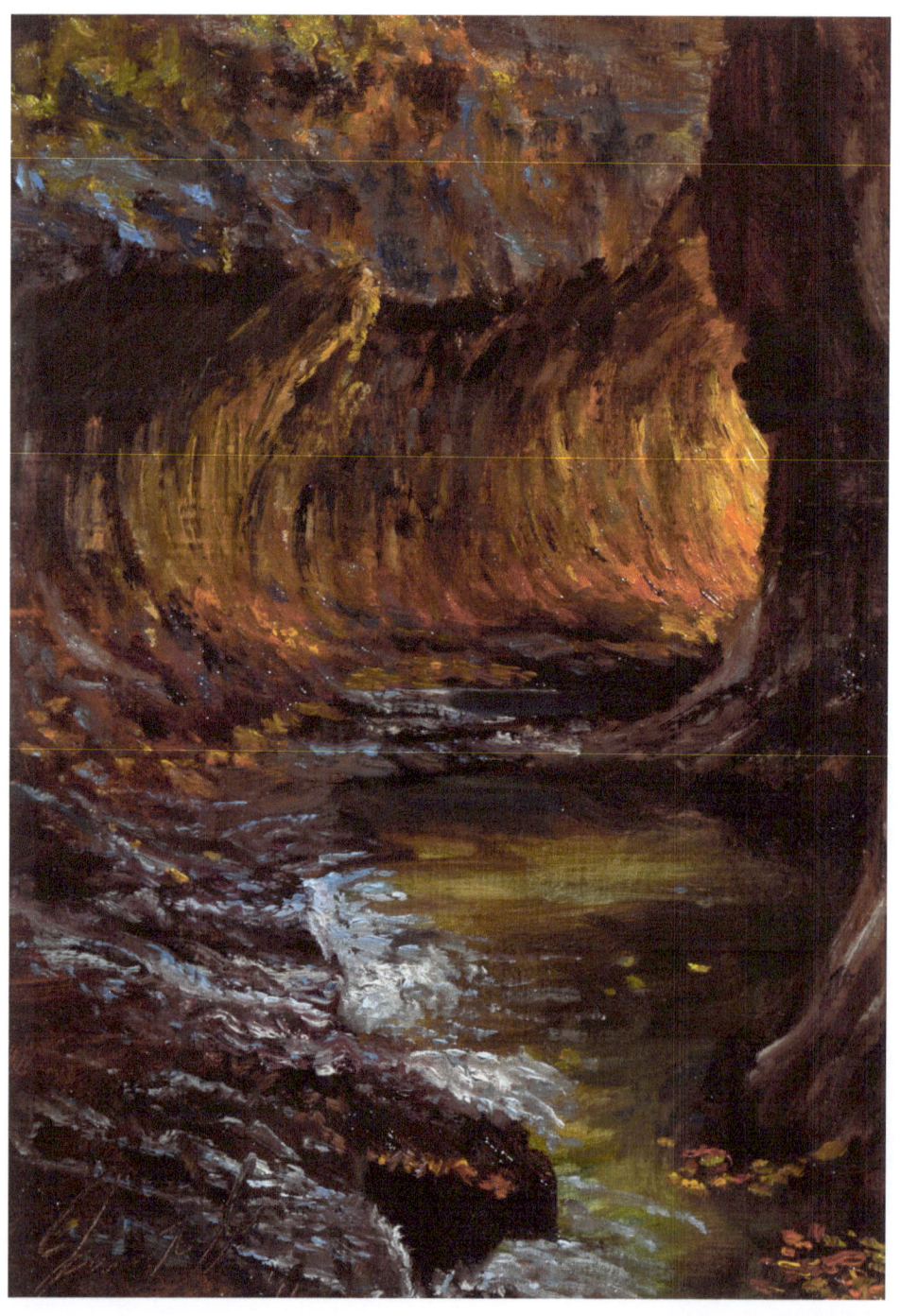

JAMES MCGREW
LAKE OSWEGO, OREGON

"Honored to carry on a legacy of painting to protect our National Parks, I strive to interpret nature with my brush, not merely copying a scene but rather conveying the feelings, emotions, weather, light, energy, movement and vision of an experience. I want the viewer to feel the wind, moisture, sunshine of the elements and feel the excitement and energy I felt while painting on location. I hope my works inspire others to love and protect our landscape/wildlife and cherish our valuable human interrelationships with each other and the environment."

James McGrew first backpacked in Yosemite at just four months old and recalls many childhood memories of family backpacking trips. He remembers always wanting to paint and photograph California's natural wonders and cultural history. Today he is best known for his oil paintings interpreting western national parks, especially Yosemite, Grand Canyon and Zion. His award winning works hang in collections around the world, and have exhibited in many solo and group shows, galleries, museums, national, and international exhibitions. He has been a top selling artist in most of his 2013-2016 invitationals.

Subway Glow
Oil
16 x 12 inches

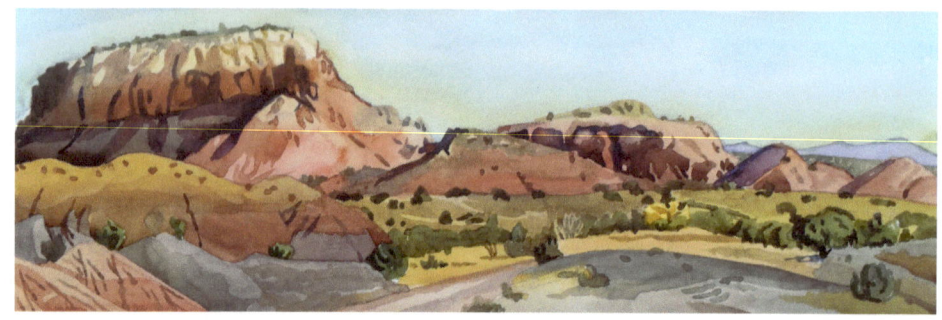

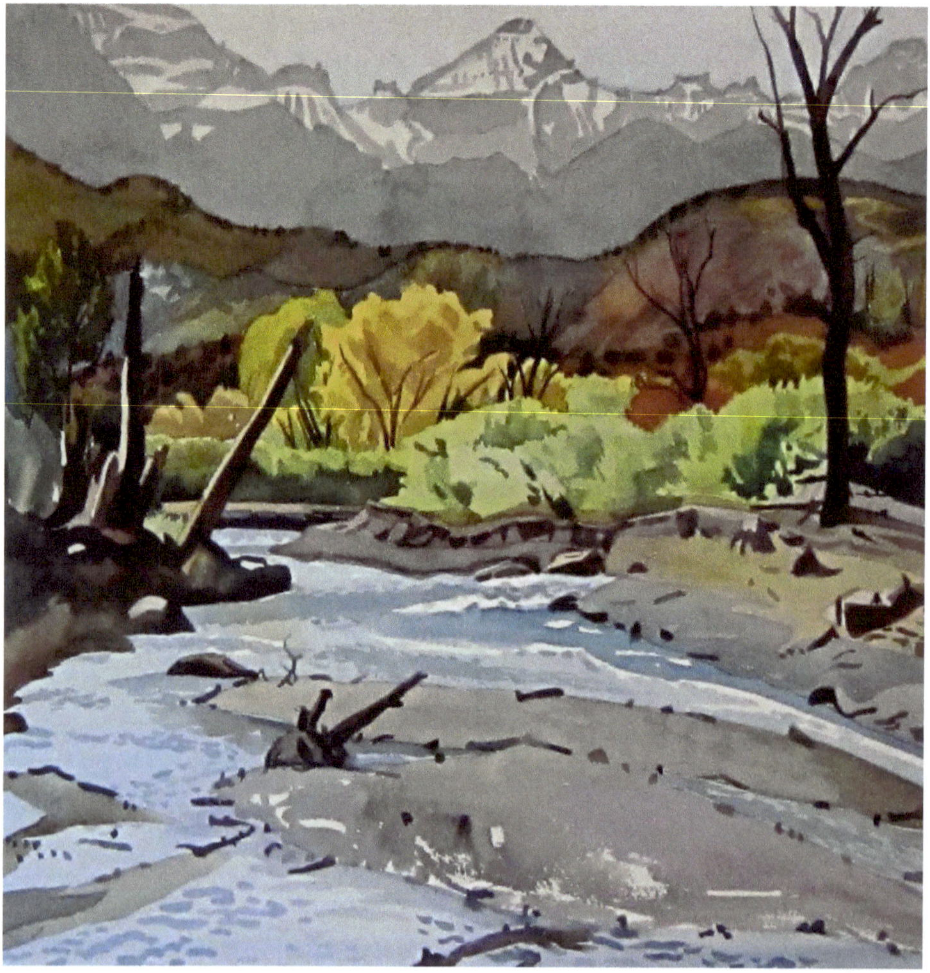

MERIDETH NEMIROV
RIDGWAY, COLORADO

"Being outside, in the moment, is so much more than making a painting of the location. It is a record, an account, of being a witness to all that is before you, capturing what occurs during that passage of time. The weather and light changing, the wind and the agitation from the mosquitoes buzzing about, the urgency to make a painting of the total experience. The visions for my work is to convey the idea that nature is not observed simply from one particular location, nor is it fixed in time, but has an invisible and intangible aspect."

Meredith Nemirov was born and raised in New York City. She received a BFA from Parson's School of Design. In New York she was a figurative painter and worked as a freelance illustrator. After her work was juried into the inaugural exhibition at the Queens Museum in 1980, she devoted herself to painting full time.

   In 1988, she moved to a small town in southwest Colorado, where she and her husband opened the Ridgway Gallery which sold antique maps, books and prints specializing in the exploration of the American West. She also started painting on location in the mountains with a focus on the tree in the landscape.

Ghost Ranch
Watercolor
7 x 21 inches

Up the Uncompahgre
Watercolor
20 x 20 inches

Corkscrew
**Pastel
38 x 14 inches**

The Layers of Capitol Reef
**Pastel
8 x 14 inches**

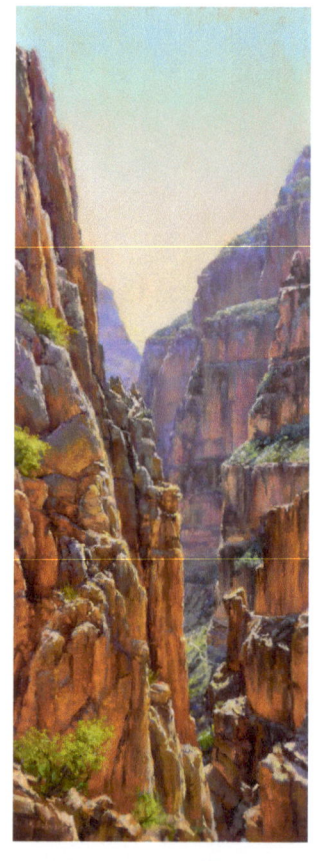
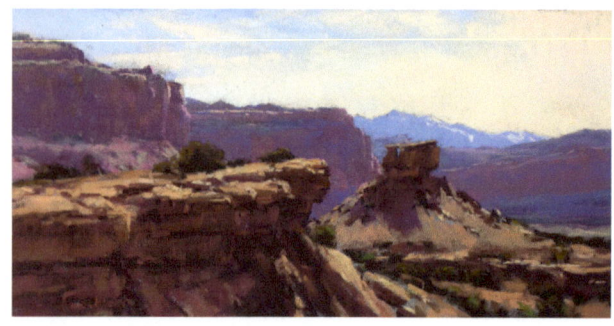
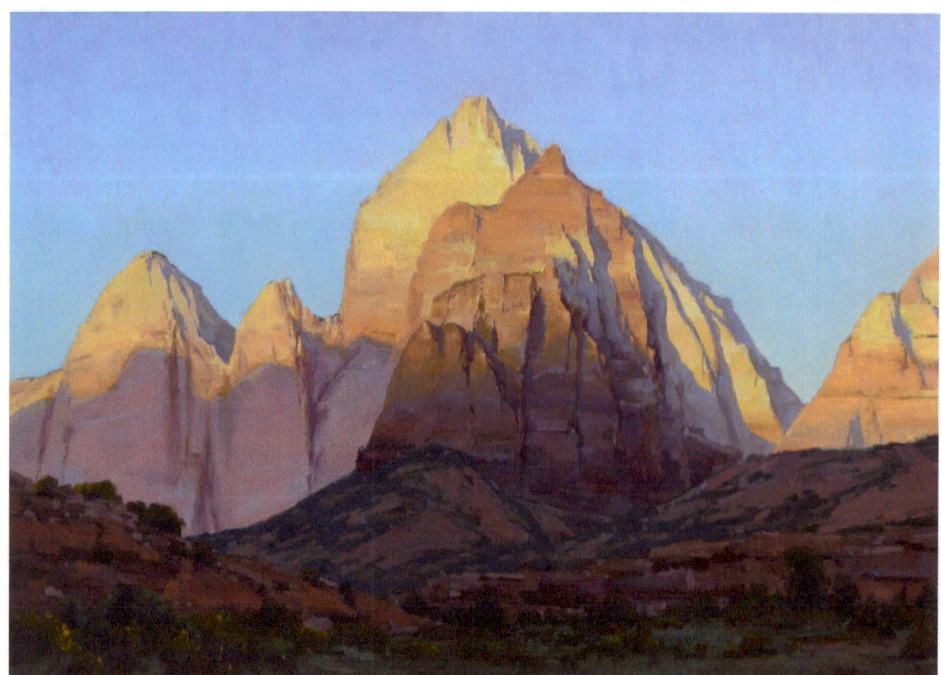

AARON SCHUERR
LIVINGSTON, MONTANA

"My art is borne out of my struggle to absorb, comprehend, and understand the natural world. . . In order to digest what I've experienced while painting in the field. I then return to the studio and paint something bigger and I take that frightening step: I invite the viewer to add his or her own story to it . . . Though painting is largely a solitary endeavor, it is never a lonely one, because I am invited to share in the ineffable mystery of beauty. . . The heart of my work is in the outdoors, absorbing the pattern of light on the landscape. Actors speak of "being in the moment," immersing themselves so totally that everything else falls away. The open air is my stage, and in the best moments, I am lost in it. I have no desire to impress you with these paintings. Rather, I strive to share my experience with honesty and without fear."

Aaron lives in Livingston, Montana with his wife and three sons. He is a signature member of The Pastel Society of America and The American Impressionist Society. He has taught at the Plein Air Convention in California and the IAPS Convention, as well as workshops across the country, and in Ireland and Morocco. He is a regular contributor to The Pastel Journal and has four instructional videos to his credit.

Zion Shadows
Oil
30 x 40 inches

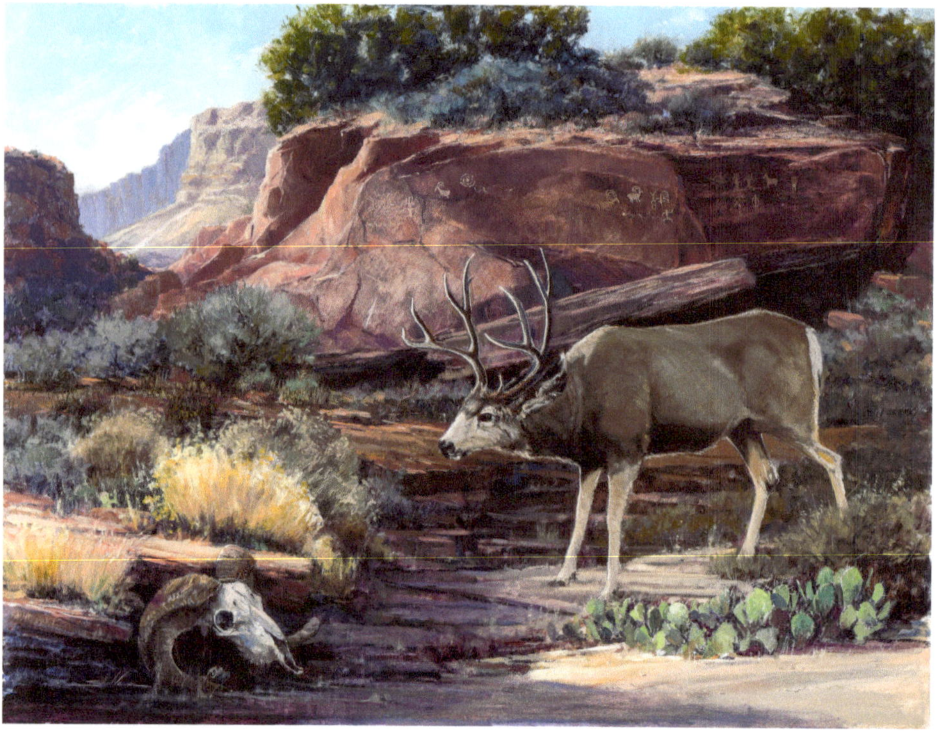

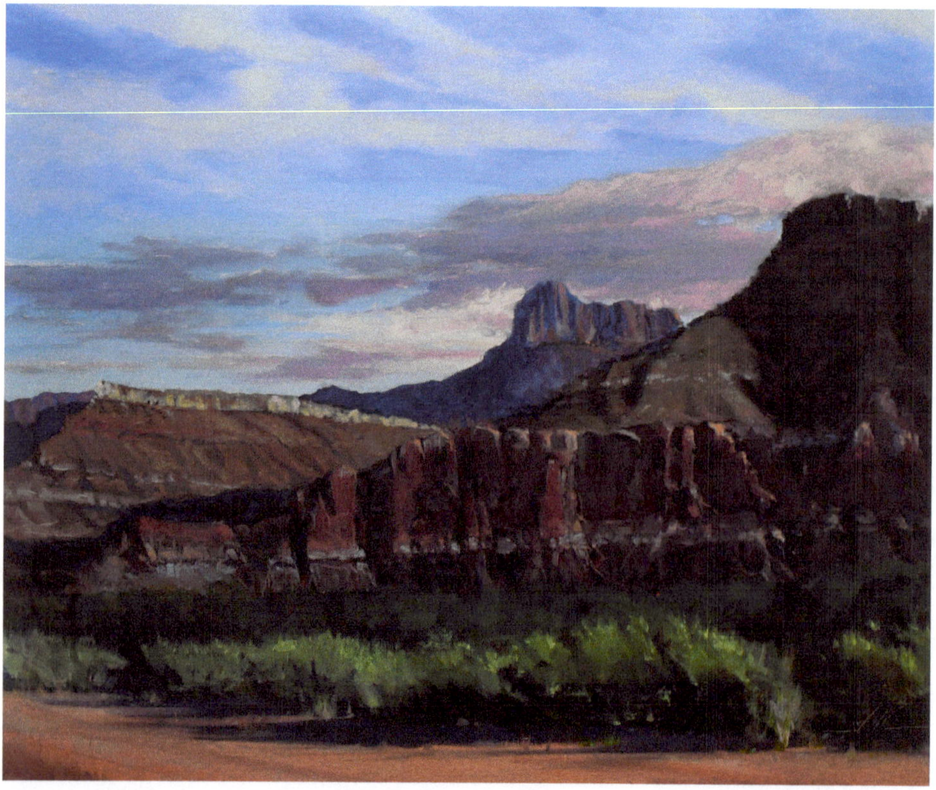

STEVE STAUFFER
MURRAY, UTAH

"Imagine the most spectacular sunrise you have ever witnessed, or the softest light that kisses the tops of the trees as a new day begins. Remember the overwhelming feeling of "ahh", as it overtakes you and leaves you speechless. That is the feeling I receive when I immerse myself into a landscape. Attempting to find that special something or place and capturing it on canvas, I share with others as they walk along with me on my journey. . . The love and passion I have to paint this magnificent world drives me each and every day. To be given a gift and . . . to sit back and say, 'There can't be a better way to celebrate our Creator's Vision!' This is what drives me and blesses my life each day!"

In 2011, Steve began his life's dream of becoming a working artist. He had painted all his life, but not until then did he realize what truly a remarkable dream it was. That dream has become a reality as he spends the majority of his time plein air painting with oils in the field as well as in the studio.

It is in Utah where he has found and experienced the passion and love of painting outdoors. As a member of Plein Air Painters of Utah, he is often found in the alpine splendor of the Rocky Mountains, or in its many national parks and red rock wonderlands.

Ancients and Old Friends
Oil
30 x 40 inches

Glimpse of Zion
Oil
16 x 20 inches

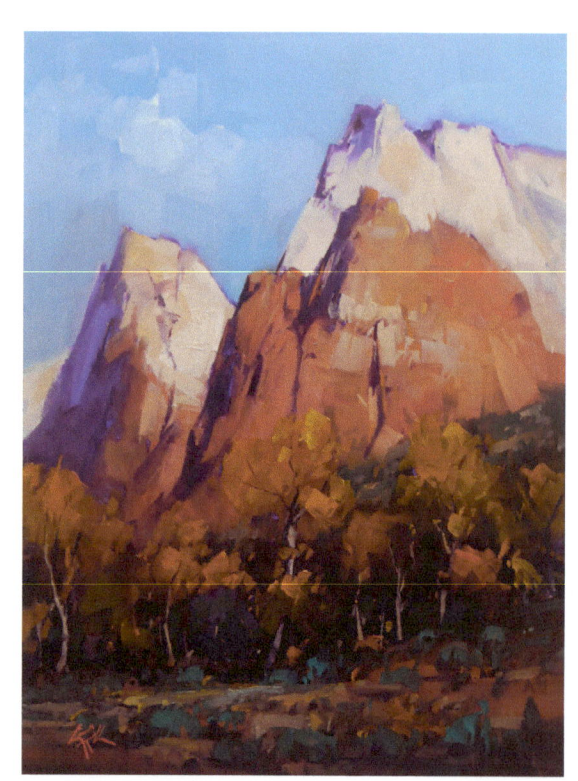

Zion Canyon Autumn
Oil
14 x 11 inches

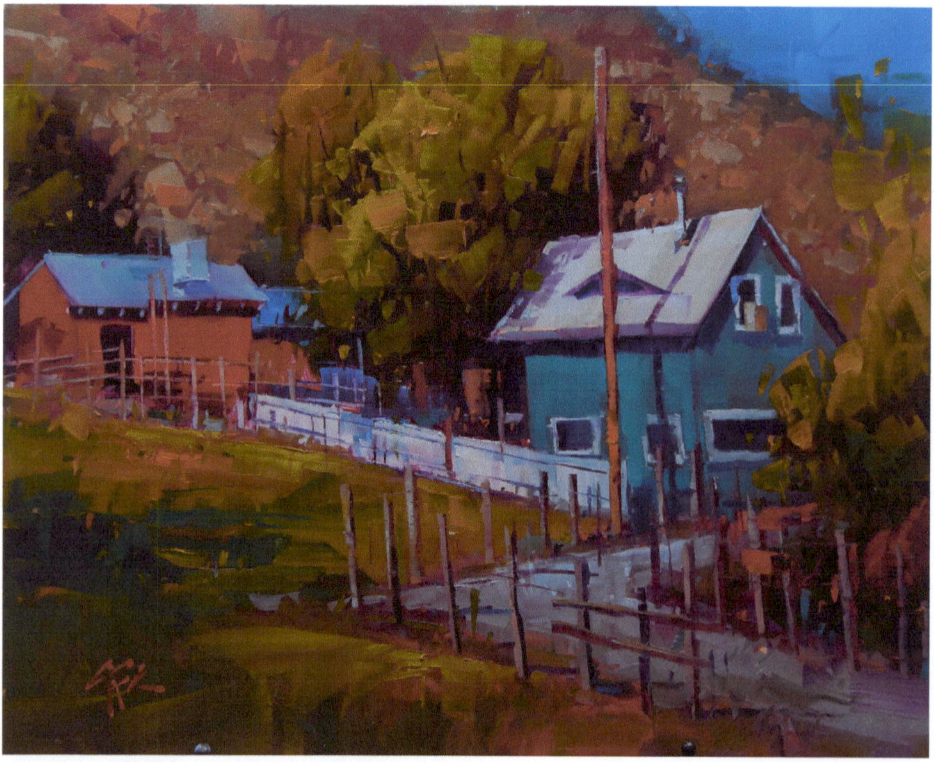

GREGORY STOCKS
COTTONWOOD, ARIZONA

"My work is an effort to create images that serve as emotional detours from the everyday world. I find the process of painting to be similar to that of writing a song. There is a basic structure or rhythm to the work. The melody comes into play in the form of color, brushwork and the expressive possibilities of process."

Gregory Stocks has been a professional exhibiting artist for over a decade and is recognized for his remarkable combination of classical representation and contemporary execution. In a light, fast pace he lays down bold, flat-edged brushstrokes using rich earth tones. His style is stark, with a clean, contemporary feel. And his scenes are a combination of memories and imagination... intended to relate not so much a place as "a place in one's heart and emotions."

Born in Lubbock, Texas, Gregory lived in California, Washington and Idaho before arriving in Utah in 1981 to attend Utah State University, where he earned a bachelor's degree in art.

Rockville Red & Blue
Oil
11 x 14 inches

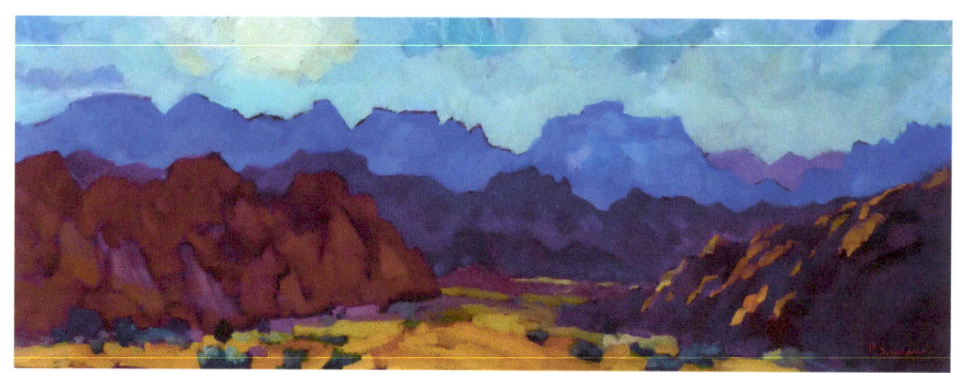

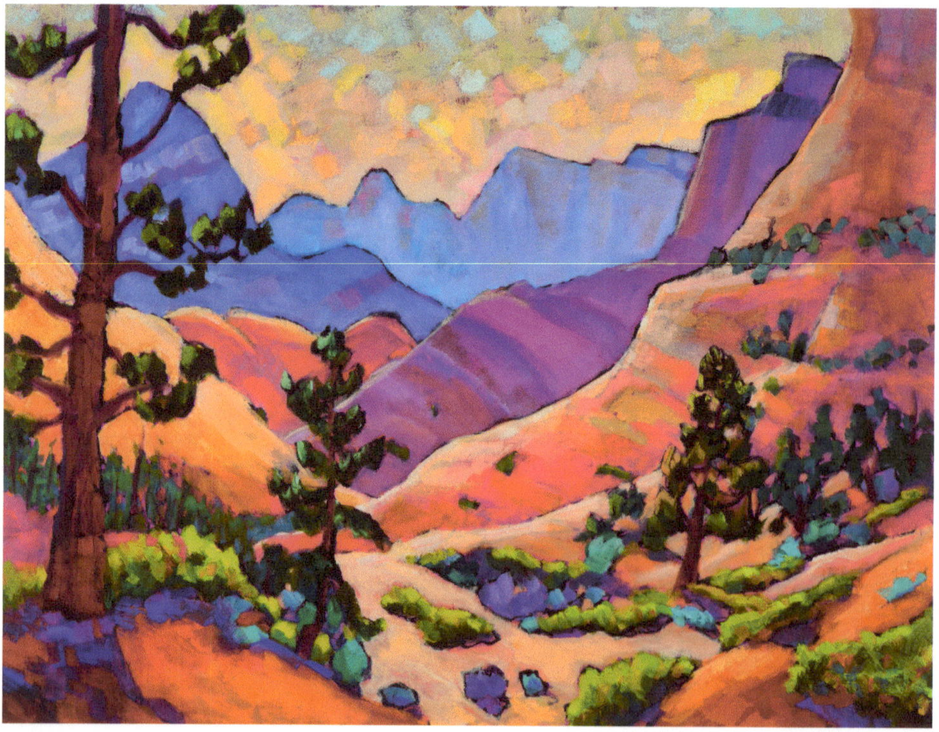

PAULA SWAIN
SALT LAKE CITY, UTAH

"A day of painting begins with finding a scene that fascinates me. I study shapes, shadows, patterns, light, colors, and map this onto the canvas. As well as growing up with both parents' painting instruction, I have continued to take multiple oil painting workshops each year to continue to learn and grow."

Paula paints plein air year round, hoping to "paraphrase the Creator's endless colors and vistas on canvas." Both of Paula's parents were art teachers, so plein air painting was part of her life from childhood. Her favorite family vacations were in the Northwest and Southwest. She went to nursing school and continues to keep her RN license current, although she paints full time now.

Kolob Terrace
Oil
9 x 24 inches

East Zion Patterns
Oil
18 x 24 inches

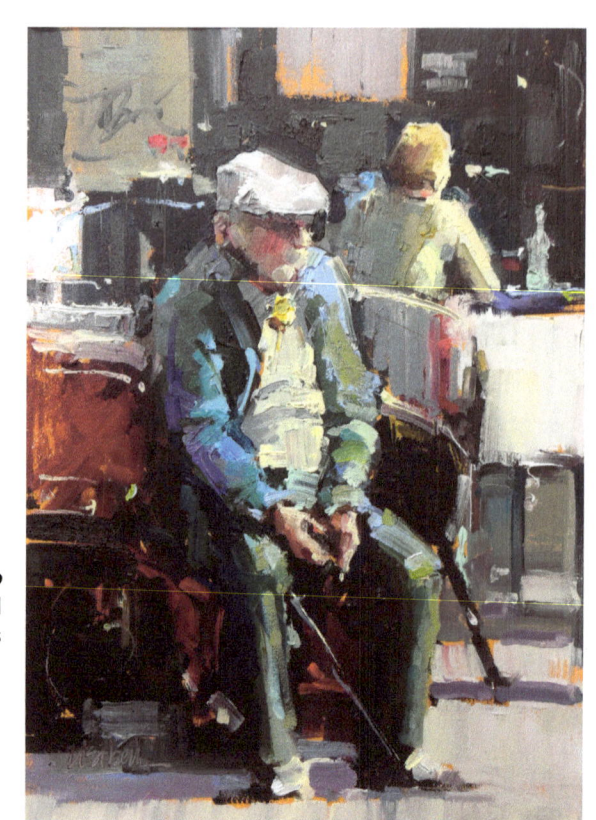

Morning Alfresco
Oil
12 x 9 inches

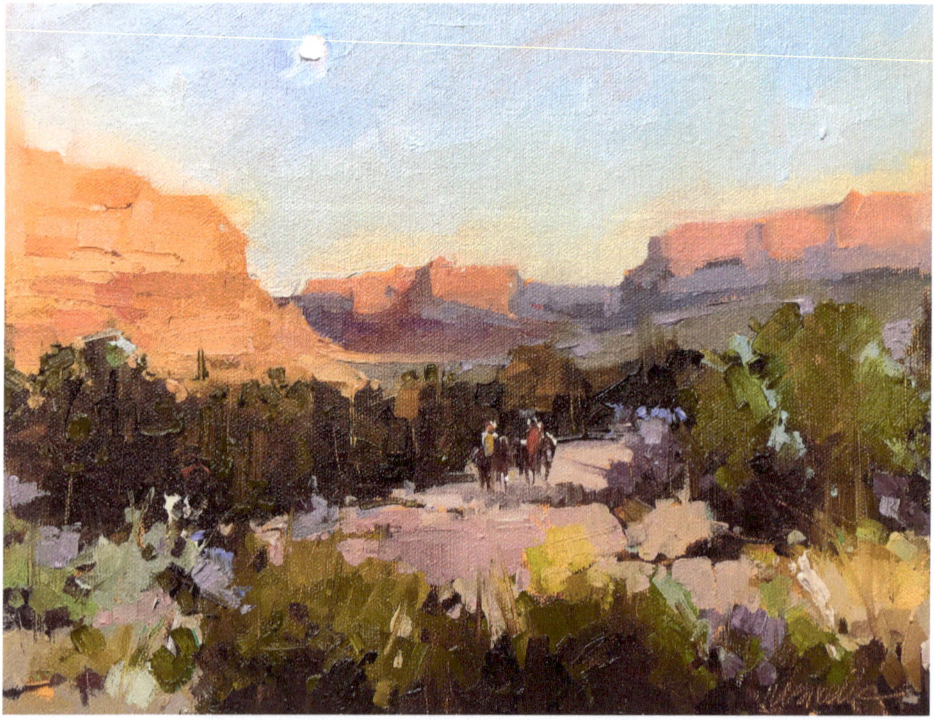

MICHELE USIBELLI
WOODWAY, WASHINGTON

"During my work in architecture, I felt deeply connected to the arts. But I truly discovered my passion when I began to explore oil painting. For me, the process of creating begins with a scene that I feel carries a certain energy and evokes an emotion. I find myself drawn to subject matter with rich colors or intriguing light. The vignettes of everyday life that inspire me to paint, regardless of whether it's a landscape, figurative work, cityscape, or portrait. It is my primary goal to have each artwork I create resonate with energy and the poetry of light. I follow my own 'rule' of painting what is truly important to me and feel very fortunate to be able to share that with all those who support and appreciate my work. There is nothing more gratifying than knowing that my work, which is so important to me, is appreciated by others."

Michele's award-winning artwork has shown in both group and solo gallery exhibitions as well as regional, national and international juried exhibitions. She has won numerous awards, most recently the Silver Medal Award at the prestigious Salmagundi Club, NYC/2015. She is honored to have her work in the permanent collection at the University of Alaska Fairbanks/Museum of the North, along with long admired historic and contemporary Alaskan artists. Recently, Michele has followed her passion to teach, conducting ongoing workshops and art demonstrations. She has proven to be a popular juror. Her artwork can be found in public and private collections throughout the world.

Toward West Temple
Oil
9 x 12 inches

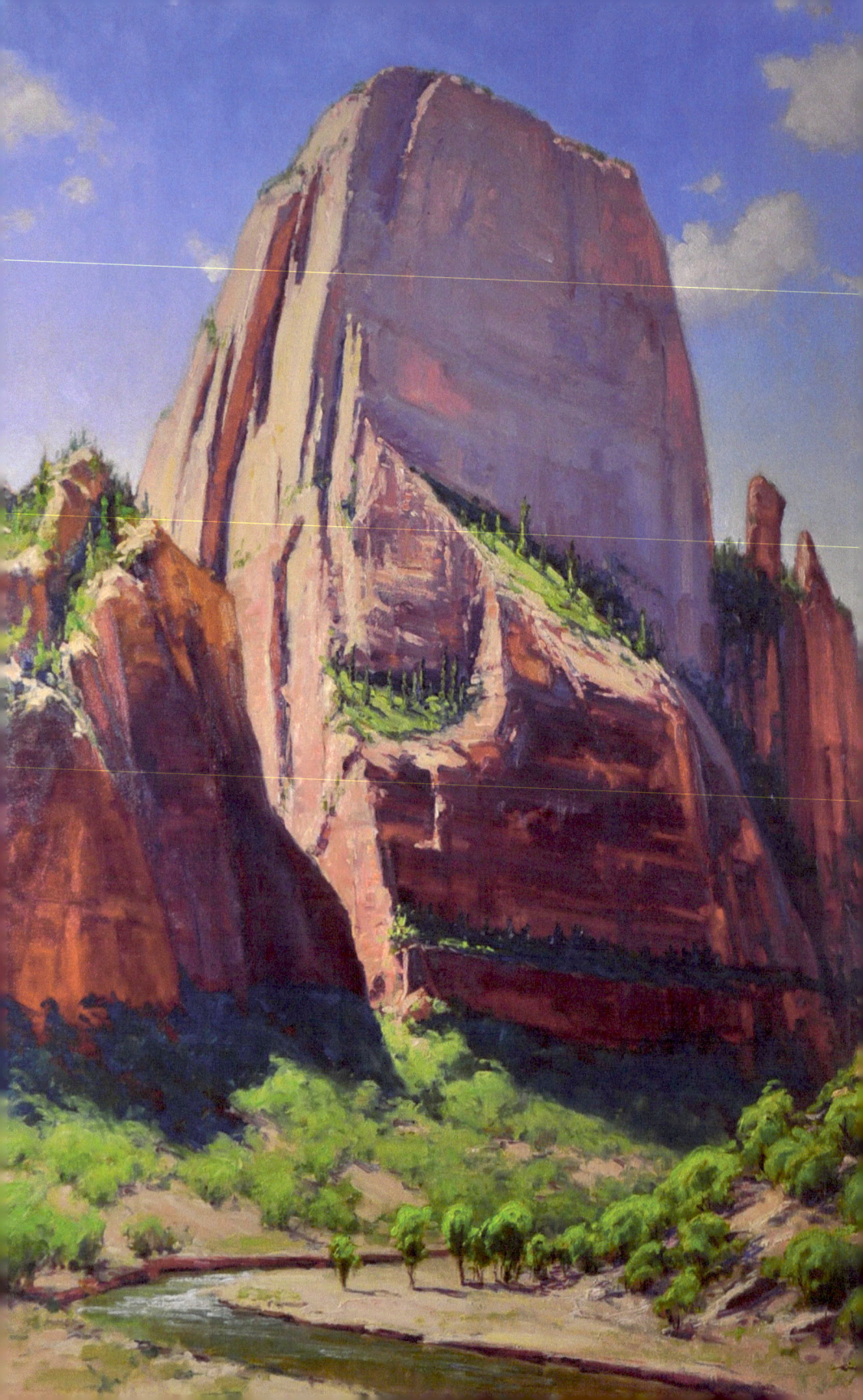

KIMBAL WARREN
MAPLETON, UTAH

"Art is the personality of one's inner self. Without that understanding, one cannot create. My art reveals how I think, feel, see, understand and even experience life. The art process is a true awareness of one's surroundings. Painting is a constant and spiritual development of problem solving. I find that I am protective of my art because it is personal to me. A good piece of art should become personal to the viewer. I paint what I see. My passion is to visit new places and capture them in the paintings I do. I hope to convey what I have seen and felt to others so that the pieces become a treasure to the owner."

Kimbal Warren received a BFA from Brigham Young University. He grew up in the Wasatch Valley where he gained his appreciation for the mountains and rural areas of the West. He has participated in many shows and continues to receive numerous awards for his work. His work is in many private and corporate collections.

    He has traveled extensively throughout the world. Warren has spent a lifetime painting, teaching and mentoring. He enjoys hiking and riding his horses in the wilderness and high country to get inspiration and material for his paintings.

Great White Throne
Oil
48 x 36 inches

Before the Narrows
Oil
24 x 18 inches

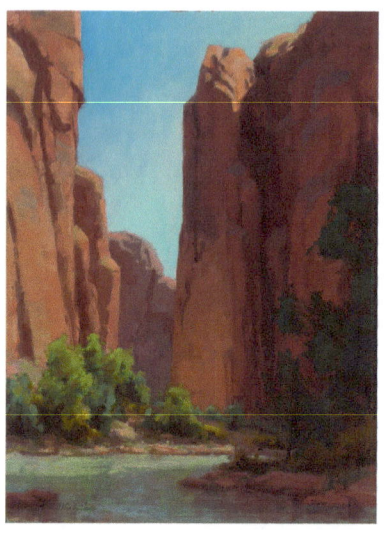
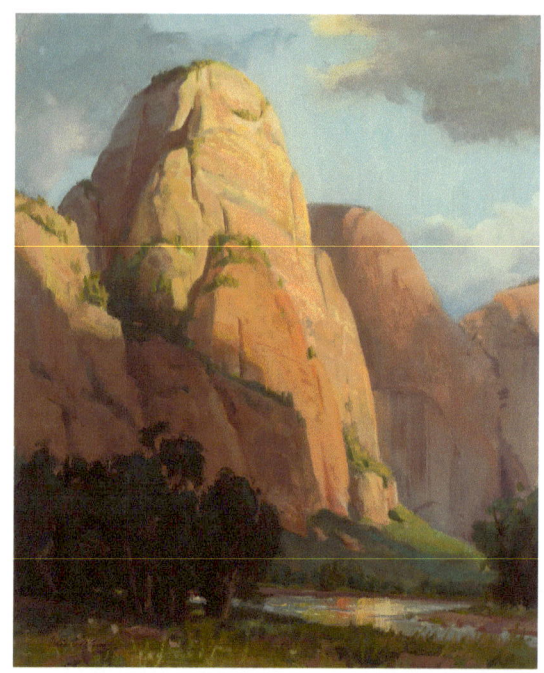

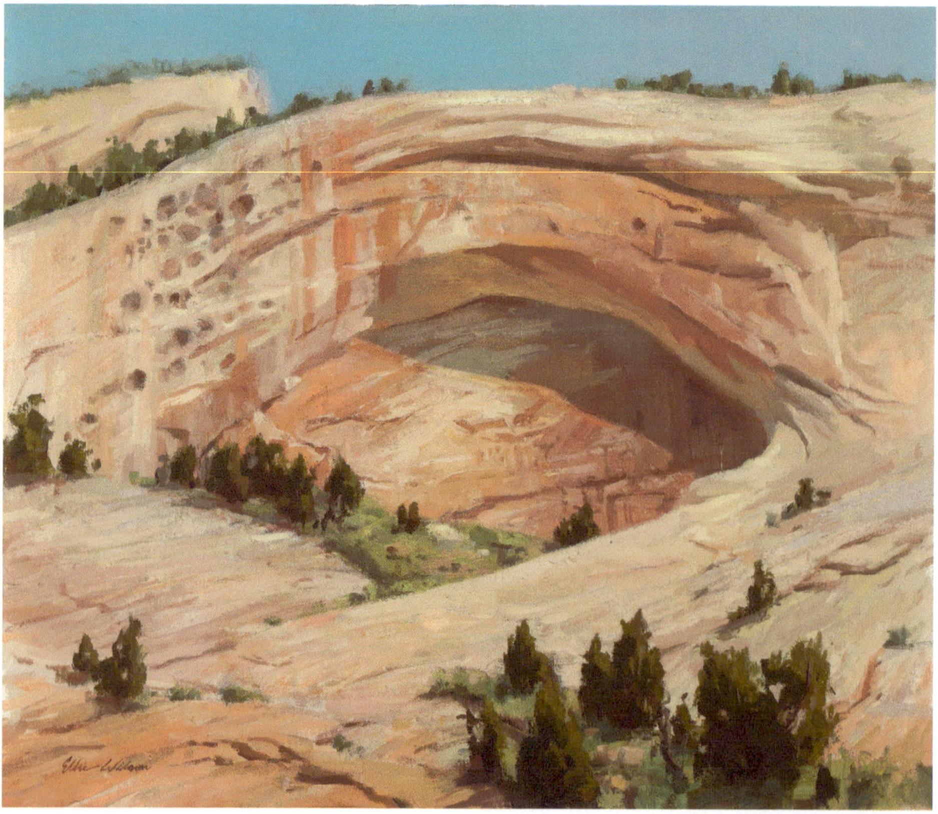

ELLIE WILSON
PROVO, UTAH

"Landscapes bring emotions, memories, and inspiration to each person. That is why I paint. My goal as an artist is to create a window through which my viewers can access the enlightenment and comfort of the natural world."

Ellie's life as an artist started at a young age, and the path to her career seems to have happened almost effortlessly. She was born and raised in the Wasatch Mountains, instilling in her a passion for nature and beauty. As she grew older she was trained in a large variety of media, but the moment she started using oil paint she never went back. Ellie started landscape painting when one of her professors at Brigham Young University invited her and some other students to go plein air painting. Standing in the open air with the mountains surrounding her and a brush in her hand "just felt right, so I kept on plein air painting and fell in love." When she graduated with a BFA from Brigham Young University in 2016, she sold out a 22-piece solo show, helping her to launch her professional career.

Temple of the Sun
Oil
24 x 20 inches

Aspiring Arch
Oil
20 x 24 inches

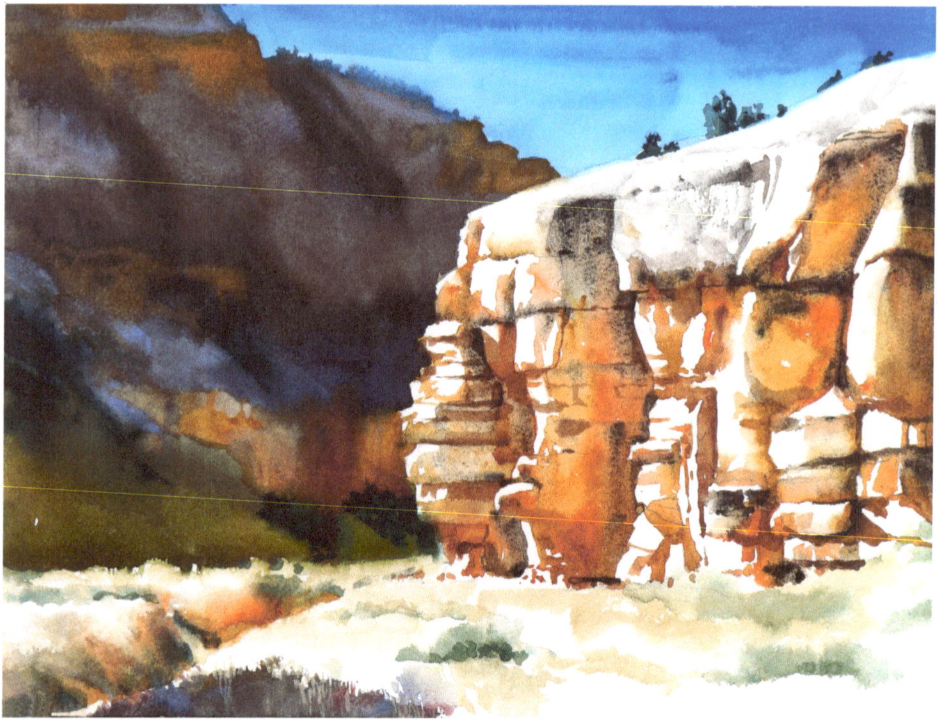

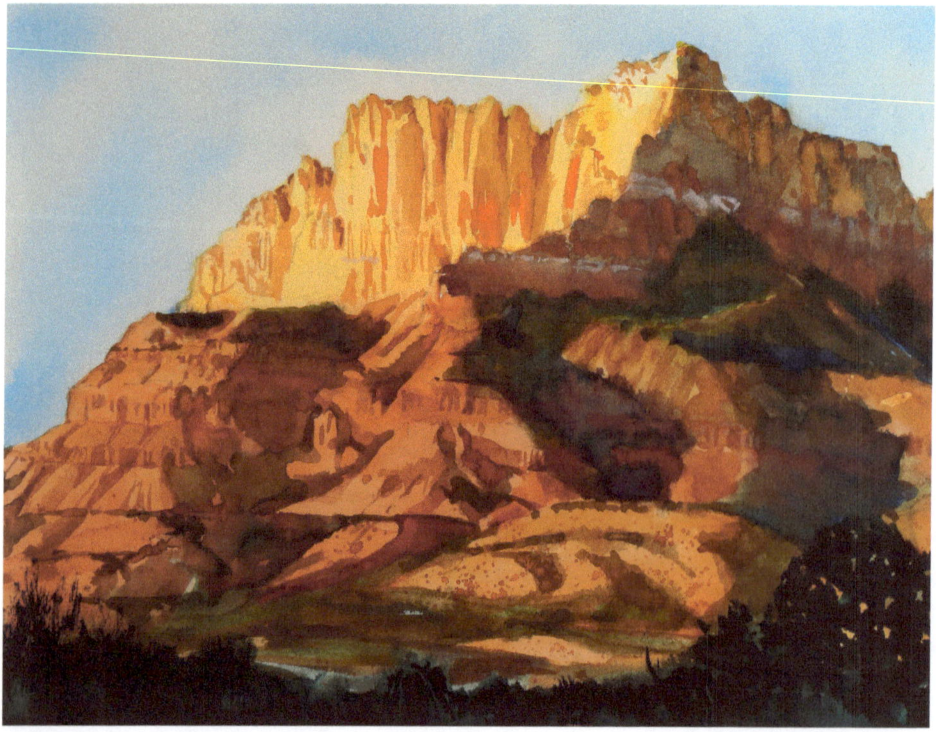

56

SUZE WOOLF
SEATTLE, WASHINGTON

"I've met my goal when I've transported the viewer into the world of the painting but that viewer remains aware my hand was on the brush. The successful painting walks a fine line between invoking reality and a collection of brush strokes."

Seattle-based Suze Woolf's work is about nature, and she does much of it in the field. She studied fine art at the University of Washington. She has won regional and national awards, such as Artist Trust's GAP grant; residencies in Zion, Glacier and North Cascades National Parks, the Grand Canyon Trust, and the Banff and Vermont Studio Centers. Her landscape paintings, portraits of individual burned trees, and artist books have been part of many exhibits nationwide

Snake Gulch
Watercolor
16 x 20 inches

Kinesava
Watercolor
16 x 20 inches

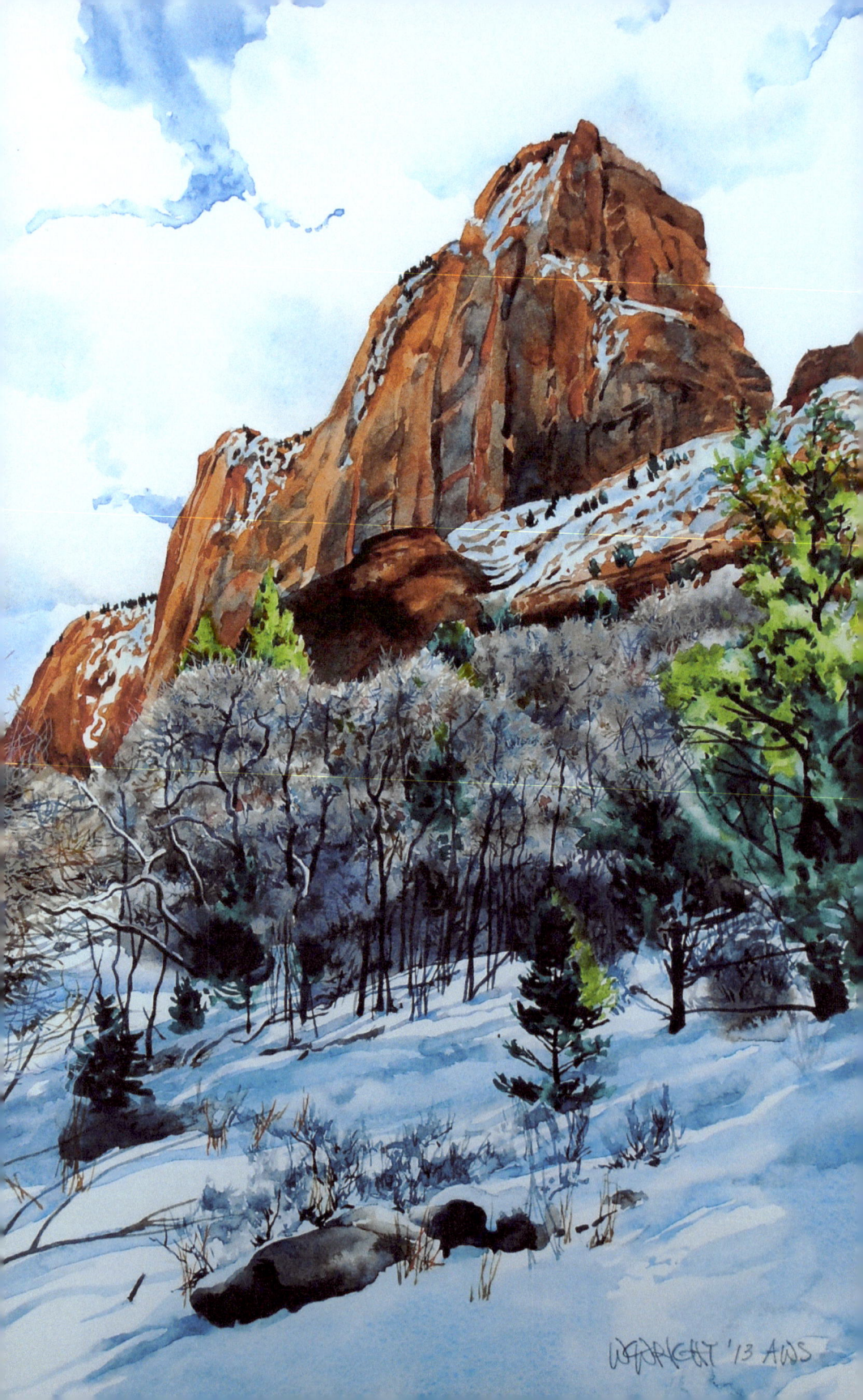

WILLIAM WRIGHT
STEVENSON, MARYLAND

"My interests are usually focused on sweeping landscapes with rolling hills, barns, and most importantly, skies. I look for quiet places that are out of the way, forgotten and run down. I am also attracted by strong light and cast shadows. I try to put some energetic movement and color in my work, but balanced by some restful places too."

William Wright has been a professional painter for over 38 years. His work has been in many galleries and national competitions throughout the U.S. including the American Watercolor Society, the Baltimore Watercolor Society, Watercolor USA, and the San Diego Watercolor Society. His work has appeared in 14 books and 6 feature magazine articles.

Taylor Creek
Watercolor
16 x 12 inches

FEATURED PAINTING DEMONSTRATION

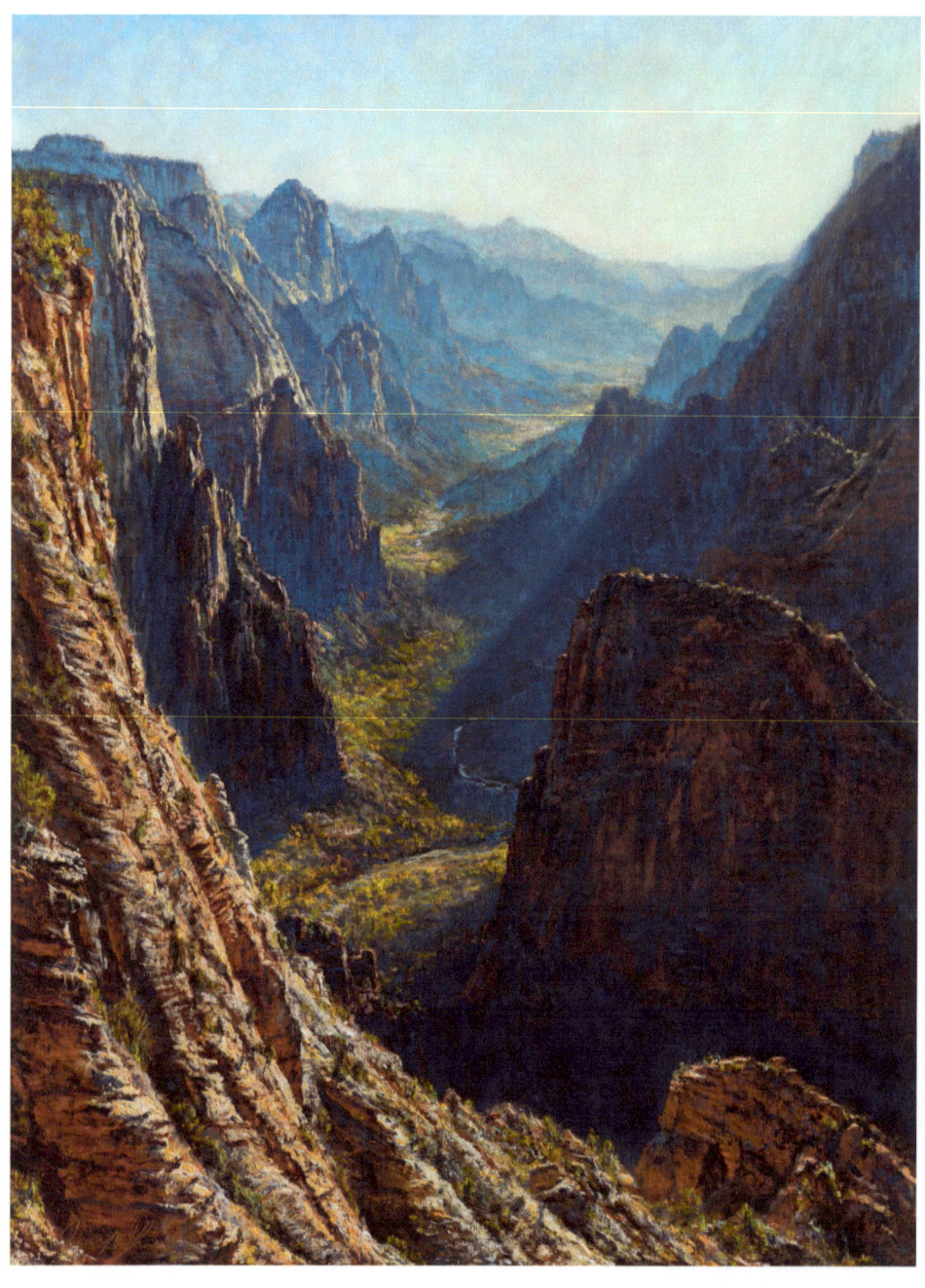

Eternal Majesty
by James McGrew

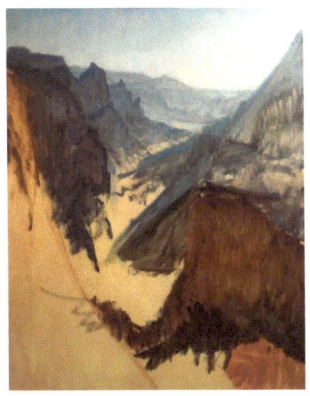 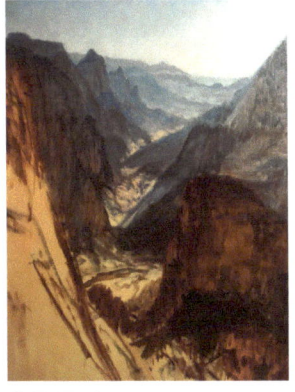 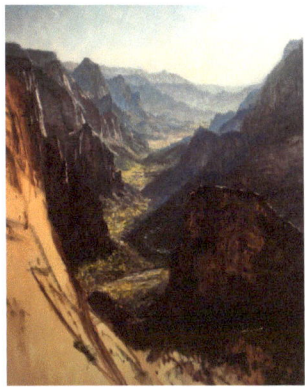

STEP 1 After a day of prep work sketches and color oil studies, I'm beginning the painting, working from my plein air work and studio studies/ sketches. I'm working on a toned ground and quickly blocking in basic shapes with transparent thinned oils.

STEP 2 Continuing blocking in shapes and shadows using thin, mostly transparent paint.

STEP 3 Working from background to foreground, beginning to refine the shapes and add opaque highlights.

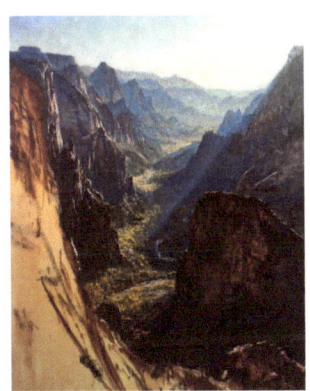 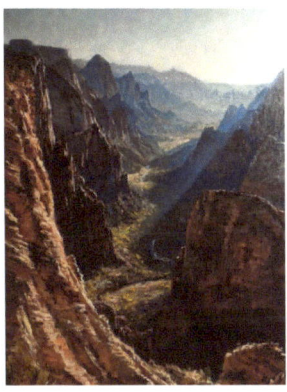 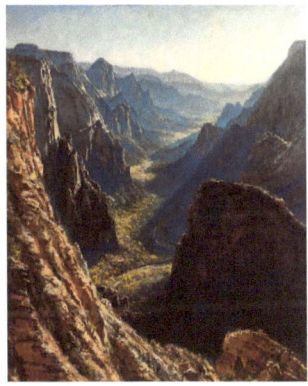

STEP 4 Further refining and working towards the foreground, constantly comparing relationships throughout.

STEP 5 Working in the foreground.

STEP 6 Further refining throughout and adding more details to the foreground.

61

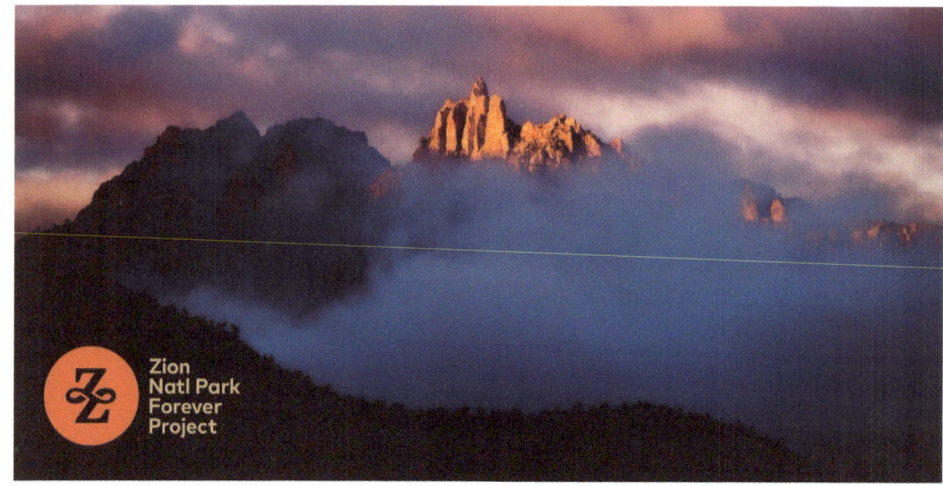

ZION FOREVER PROJECT– MAKING A DIFFERENCE NOW AND FOREVER

Preservation • Education • Visitor Experience • Sustainability

Zion National Park contains some of the most sacred and important canyon country in the world and has been a sanctuary for more than ten thousand years. It is the fifth most heavily visited national park in the country. As the park's official nonprofit partner, the Zion Natl Park Forever Project provides private support for projects that preserve the integrity of the Zion experience now, and for generations to come.

While federal appropriations and entrance fees support the park's basic day to day operations and maintenance needs, the Forever Project provides the park's margin of excellence through the programs it leads and those it helps to fund.

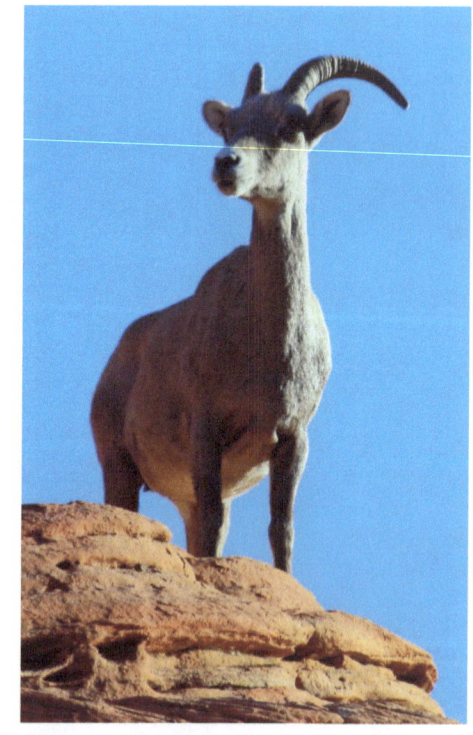

Above: bighorn sheep preservation.
Right: Concrete-to-Canyons program.

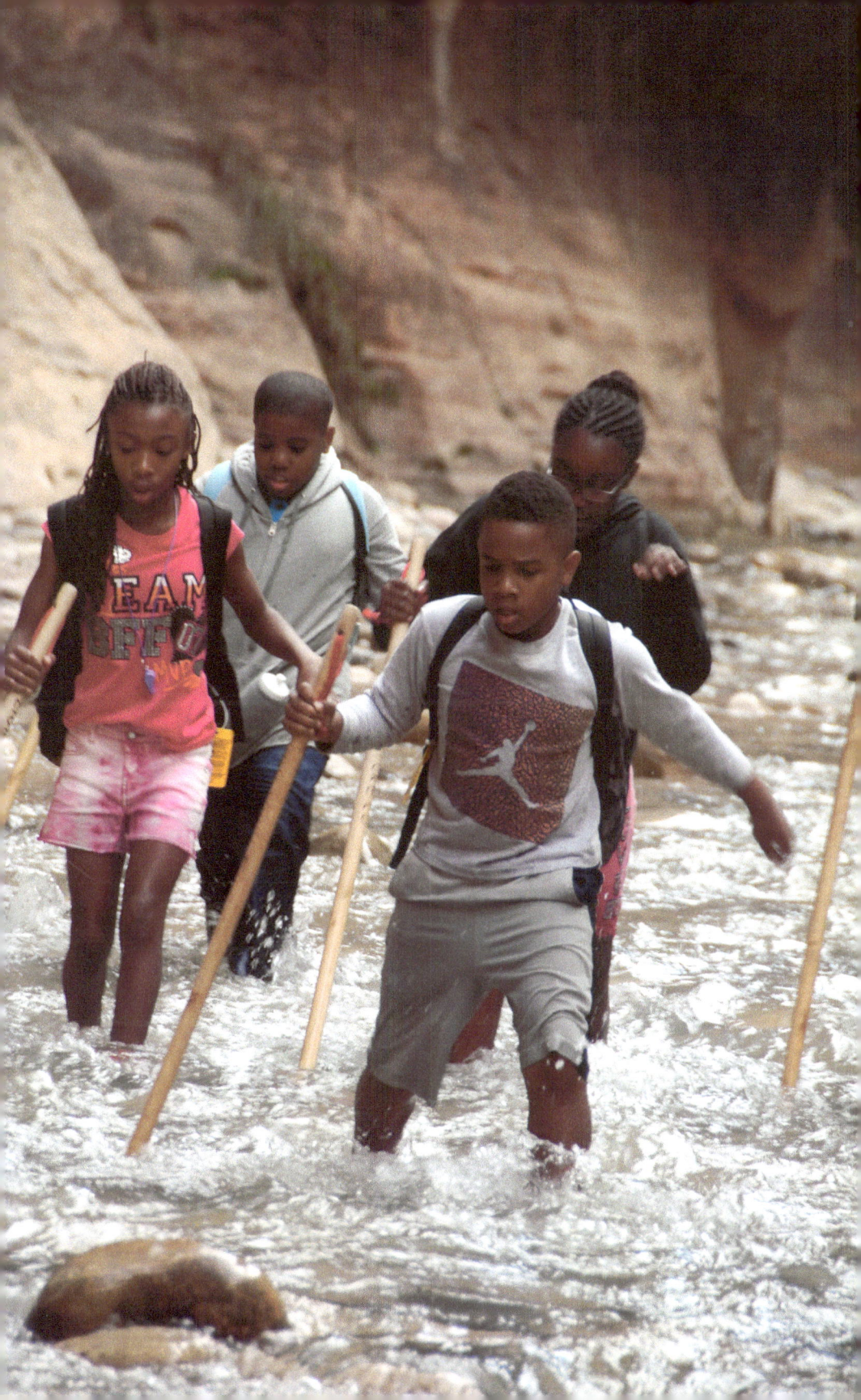

The Forever Project park stores provide books, maps, outdoor gear, and other interpretive products that are developed and selected to articulate and support the Park's Interpretation Plan – providing another layer of connection for the park visitor, inspiring them to become park stewards and champions.
The Forever Project curates and leads more than fifty coures a year through its Field Program, offering visitors a deeper understanding of the park's natural and cultural resources.

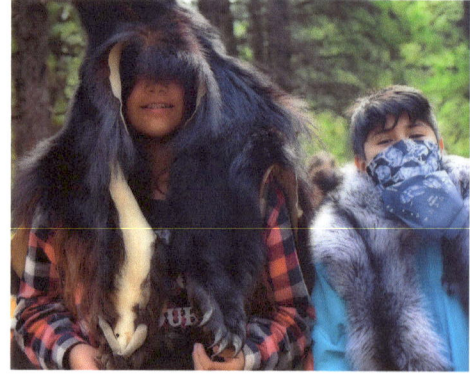

Camp Kwiyumuntsi strengthens cultural connections for Paiute youth.

The Forever Project wishes to extend its deep appreciation to the art patrons, sponsors, contributors, our National Park Service partner, and the exceptional and generous artists who make this event possible.

We invite you to join us in our work today at zionpark.org or at any Forever Project Park Store or by calling 1-435-772-3264.

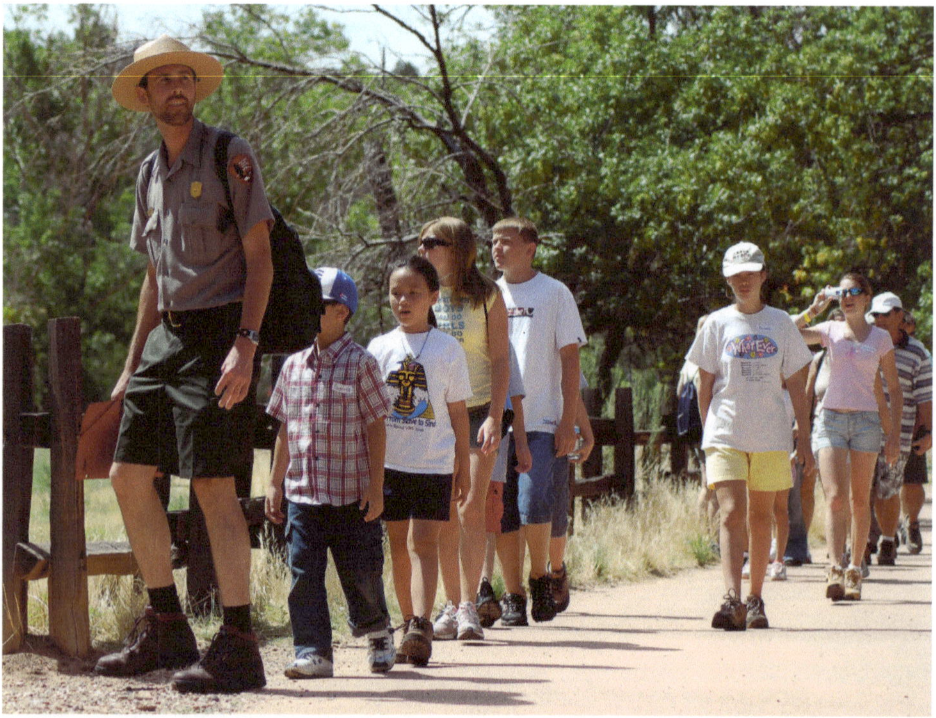

The Junior Ranger program engages thousands of children and their families.

www.ingramcontent.com/pod-product-compliance
Lightning Source LLC
Chambersburg PA
CBHW040235220526
45473CB00001B/245